MARRYING
AN
OLDER
MAN

MARRYING AN OLDER MAN

Maggie Jones

PIATKUS

Copyright © 1993 Maggie Jones

First published in 1993 by
Judy Piatkus (Publishers) Limited,
5 Windmill Street, London W1P 1HF

The moral right of the author has been asserted

*A catalogue record for this book is available
from the British Library*

ISBN 0-7499-1139-5

Designed by Sue Ryall

Typeset by Computerset, Harmondsworth, Middlesex
Printed and bound in Great Britain by Mackays of Chatham PLC

CONTENTS

INTRODUCTION

When a woman marries an older man – a man who is at least 10 years older – she is probably going to have to justify it in the eyes of the world. People who might think twice about other more personal questions do not seem to hesitate before asking, 'How old is your husband?' . . . 'How old were you when you got married?' . . . and the probing questions designed to find out, 'Why?' Usually there are other unspoken thoughts: 'Is she marrying him for his money? Is she marrying him because she is seeking security? Is she looking for a father figure?' And always in the back of their minds, 'Will it last?'

Anyone who marries an older man will come up against these reactions sooner or later. It would be naive to think that women who marry older men are not in a special situation. You may say, 'But I never think about his age; it's not an issue with us.' Even if that is so, it will be an issue to everybody else, and it's important to know how to deal with the comments that will come your way.

Obviously these issues apply as much to women who live with older men as those who marry them. But while there are many women who have an older lover – often married to another woman – most couples where there is a larger age gap choose to formalise their relationship through marriage. As one woman said, 'With a twenty-year age gap I felt there was enough against us without remaining unmarried. We both felt we needed a public statement of our commitment to one another and that this would help other people, especially our families, to come to terms with our relationship.'

When a marriage to an older man is going well, and this is obvious to the outside world, people will still ask, 'But what about when he's older? How will you feel about it then?' If it's going badly, people who warned you about the pitfalls will say, 'I told you so.' The greater the age gap, the more people will question it; a difference of 10 years is much more acceptable to people than one of 20 years, and an age gap of 30 years or more seems really beyond the pale.

The rich and the famous

Marriages of younger women and older men are often in the public eye. This is because a lot of people in showbusiness and the media have much younger spouses. Often this is the usual stereotype of the successful man who can take his pick of the attractive younger women who come his way; and the younger woman who achieves fame and success through her relationship with an older, more powerful man.

Many of these marriages cause intense public speculation. There was the case of Jacqueline Kennedy and Aristotle Onassis; was she marrying him for his lifestyle or for love? Similar questions were asked when Grace Kelly married Prince Rainier of Monaco. When rumours first circulated about the state of the marriage between Prince Charles and Diana, much of the speculation centred around the 12-year age gap and whether Charles, prematurely aged by the weight of his role as heir to the throne, could have much in common with his young wife who liked pop music and, it was rumoured, roller skating down the corridors of Buckingham Palace.

In the world of film and television, there are many examples of young beautiful wives and older husbands. Actress Sarah Miles has twice married the playwright Robert Bolt, who is 17 years her senior. Actor Rod Steiger, 67, has been married to beautiful blonde Paula Ellis, 32, for five years. TV star Paul Daniels is married to his assistant Debbie McGee, who is 20 years younger than him. John Hurt, aged 51, has a new wife, Jo, aged 33;

Patricia Hodge is 46 and her husband Peter Miller 61. Bo Derek is 34 and her husband is 65. The world of pop, too, has many such marriages; Rod Stewart 47, married model Rachel Hunter, 23, in December 1990. The brief marriage of Bill Wyman of the Rolling Stones, then aged 52, to 19-year-old Mandy Smith captured the headlines.

Politics is another sphere in which affairs and second marriages abound. Politicians obliged to leave their wives behind in their constituencies fall prey to the temptations offered by the young female secretaries and researchers who are turned on by politics and politicians. Some merely have affairs, which can then damage or even ruin their career. Others marry. Power is the ultimate aphrodisiac for many women.

Then there are the men in the world of the arts like Roger Vadim who transformed first Brigitte Bardot, then Jane Fonda and a string of other young women into stars. Such relationships seem doomed to failure; if the chief attraction of a wife is that she is young and beautiful, how long will the marriage last when the wife begins to lose her youthful appeal and the man has sufficient wealth to attract another, more beautiful, young replacement? And what about the wives? Are they just after the money, or will it matter to them when the man becomes too frail to continue with the social whirl which seems to play a major part in such relationships?

It seems fairly certain that, like most show-biz marriages, very few of these relationships will last. John De Lorean, the ill-fated car manufacturer, who moved in the international jet set, married three beautiful women, the second and third, Kelly Harman and model Christina Ferrare, over 20 years his junior. He says, 'My three wives are still the most beautiful women I've ever seen in my entire life. That's great if you want to put somebody on a shelf and look at them, but it's not exactly the right criterion for a happy marriage.'

In America recently much has been written about the phenomenon of the rich and famous casting off their long-standing and now ageing wives for beautiful young women – known as 'trophy wives'. Research by Dr Frank Pitman, professor of psychology at the University of Georgia, showed that more and more men are seeking women 'who look like centrefolds', so that they themselves can appear more potent to their clients and business rivals. 'Men who collect trophy wives don't look for friendship, support or even comfort in marriage,' Pitman is quoted as saying. 'Their wives are as exchangeable and disposable as cars. They are merely status symbols.'

Ordinary people

Can we compare these marriages in any way with those of more ordinary mortals? According to figures collected by the Office for Population Censuses and Surveys, there are over 40,000 marriages every year in which the men are at least 10 years older than their wives.

Of the 42,900 marriages with an age difference of 10 years or more (in the last year for which such figures are available, 1989), by far the biggest number were women aged 20-24 marrying men aged 30-34. There were 11,143 such marriages. Marriages of women aged 25-29 marrying men aged 35-39 numbered just over 7,000.

Where the age gap is even bigger however, marriages are much more rare. There were only about 13,500 marriages with an age gap of about 20 years. The majority, 1,053 of these, were marriages between women aged 20-24 and men aged 40-44. When the gap gets to 30 years the numbers are tiny; only 592 men married women 30 years younger, and there are only a handful of marriages where the gap is 40 years or more. For example, only 43 marriages took place between women aged 20-24 and men aged 55-59. Only five women under 20 married men over 55.

There is evidence that the number of marriages between older men and younger women is actually decreasing. The greater freedom of choice of spouse, and the fact that it is considered less important for the man to have accumulated property or established himself in his chosen field before marriage, has led to a decrease in the age difference between husband and wife and an increase in the proportion of marriages between young people of the same age.

One study carried out in 1950 showed that 74 per cent of men aged 40-49 had married younger women, while only 40 per cent of the men aged 29 or younger had done so. The author commented that 'before the First World War it was widely believed that the man should be 5 to 10 years older than the woman; especially in the middle classes, other behaviour was viewed as a deviation.'

Arranged marriages

In primitive societies, marriage tended to take place soon after puberty; a survey of hunter-gathering societies showed that the usual age of marriage was 15. Marriages of young women take place in many societies, especially where the match is usually arranged by the parents, and here large age gaps are not uncommon. In the West, marriages tend to take place later. There has been a long trend in industrialised countries towards a higher average age of marriage.

Before the twentieth century, marriages of girls aged 15-17 were not disapproved of provided the husband was sufficiently wealthy. In the West, marriage was not thought to be properly based on 'free courtship' till the nineteenth century, and many young women were married off to older men to make a 'good match'.

Increasing freedom of choice

According to Lawrence Stone's classic work, *The Family, Sex and Marriage in England 1500-1800*, women of the upper landed classes usually married at about 20 in the late sixteenth century, rising to about 22-23 in the late seventeenth and eighteenth. With men, there was a clear distinction between the son and heir and his younger brothers. The usual age of first marriage for heirs was about 21-22 in the sixteenth century, rising to 24-26 in the seventeenth and early eighteenth and 27-29 in the late eighteenth to early nineteenth centuries. This trend is thought to be due to the greater willingness of parents to let their children choose their spouse, allowing them more time to make their decision, and the increasing amount of time spent acquiring further education.

Younger sons married later than their eldest brothers, and by the eighteenth century were usually marrying in their early to middle thirties, normally choosing partners who were 10 years or so younger. This was because they had to save enough money from their profession to support their wives and maintain the lifestyle to which they had been accustomed.

Among the middle and lower classes marriage took place very late from the fifteenth century onward, with an average of 27-29 for men and 25-27 for women. This was because when couples married they were supposed to set up house on their own, which usually meant saving enough money to live independently of the parents.

Death of one spouse – often the wife dying as a result of childbirth – brought an early end to many marriages, the average duration being about 20 years, rising to 30 at the end of the eighteenth century for the landed gentry. Remarriage was very common, with about a quarter of all marriages being remarriages for either bride or groom. A couple marrying during this period of history had less than a 50 per cent chance of being together for more than a year or two after their children had left home. In the words of Lawrence Stone, 'It looks very much as if modern divorce is little more than a functional substitute for death.'

Modern marriages

Remarriage is all too common in modern day Britain; one-third of all marriages are remarriages. Despite the frequency of divorce – one in three marriages – about 80 per cent of people divorcing before the age of 30 marry again within five years. In Britain, about 90 per cent of men marry younger women in their first marriage, 75 per cent in their second. On average, second partners are about four years younger than their predecessors.

In the United States, around three out of four husbands of all ages are older than their wives. But this age gap, at least in first marriages, has grown smaller over the years: while the median age difference in 1890 was 4.1 years, by 1978 it had dropped to 2.4 years.

One implication of the convention that wives should be younger than their husbands is that it tended to enforce the inferior or 'minority' status of women, because being senior in age usually carried with it a certain amount of power and authority. But, although many marriages with an age gap are still between younger women marrying their bosses, is this necessarily true today? Do younger wives, more than others, defer to or feel in the shadow of their older spouses?

Today, as we have seen, while marriages with a 10-year gap are fairly common, gaps of 20 years or more are comparatively rare. The difference between these marriages now and those which occurred in the past is that today's age gap marriages are freely chosen. How, then, do these marriages fare? Do they lead to happiness or to problems later on? These and many other questions are dealt with in the following chapters. Of course, every marriage is different, and every individual, young or old, brings their own hopes, expectations, fears and problems into a relationship. The many interviews carried out in researching this book show how difficult it is to generalise about relationships between younger women and older men.

Marriages to older men seemed neither happier nor unhappier than any other marriages, though perhaps there were some significant differences. In marriages to older men, as in other marriages, those which were happier were the marriages in which there was realism rather than romanticism; open and free communication between the two partners; shared experiences in common; and a desire to compromise and make the relationship work. Indeed, marriages to older men tended to score better in these areas than many other marriages because the couples tended to have thought through possible problems more carefully, and because the consequences of failure seemed higher.

This book looks at celebrity marriages only in passing. It concentrates on the marriages of thousands of ordinary couples in which the man is considerably older, and the much rarer marriages where there is an age gap of 20-30 years or more. We

will look at the special problems and rewards in such relationships; and how, if you are in love with or contemplating
marrying an older man, you can avoid some of the pitfalls and
prepare yourself for the kinds of problems which may lie ahead.

Chapter 1

THE APPEAL OF
THE OLDER MAN

'A man's looks often improve with age, seldom a
woman's. He thought: a man should never love a
woman less than twenty years younger than himself.
In that way he can die before the vision fades.'

DR EDUARDO PLARR, IN GRAHAM GREENE'S
The Honorary Consul

'A man, though grey-haired, can always get a wife,
but a woman's time is short.'

ARISTOPHANES' *Lysistrata*

What is it that makes older men more attractive to women
than the other way round? Why do so many more women
marry men who are substantially older than vice versa?

Part of the answer is rooted in our biology. Women are at their
most fertile in their twenties; by their early thirties fertility is
already decreasing, and by the end of their thirties many women
have problems conceiving. In addition, the risks of pregnancy and
childbirth increase with age, as do the risks to the child, so that
having a child over the age of 40 becomes something to contemp-
late very carefully. In contrast, men retain their fertility into old

age; although there is a decline in fertility, many men continue to be capable of fathering a child well into their seventies.

One argument, or prejudice, sometimes advanced against marriage with an older man is that it is somehow 'unnatural', because 'in nature' nubile females mate with the younger, strongest males who will best be able to protect them and be least likely to be killed or die while they are bringing up their young.

Like much pseudo-science, this theory turns out to be wrong. Among most species of primates, the animals most closely related to man, males mature both physically and socially several years later than females, and naturalists have observed that the single most important indication of high status in the primate community is maturity, not fighting ability or social aggressiveness.

Full social maturity amongst primates takes even longer to attain than full adult size, with 'leader' males usually aged 14-25, while females reach breeding age in 4-5 years. The older and more dominant males appear most attractive to the females, and the oldest males are the most likely to succeed in mating at the female's fertile time. The males who father the most offspring are those who live the longest. The young males, being more aggressive, are more likely to die or be injured through fighting and hunting. Similarly, among humans it is young men who are sent into battle at wartime.

Fertility

Women's fertility ends rather suddenly with the change of life or menopause, which occurs on average at the age of 48. The physical changes which take place at the menopause mean that women age more suddenly than men. This is not to say that women beyond the menopause become instantly unattractive to men; not at all. But many women say they notice a difference in the way men view them beyond a certain age, and that this tends to happen quite suddenly.

Physical attraction

Another factor is that society tends to judge women much more by physical appearance than it does men. Women pay far more attention to clothing, make-up and hair care, to make themselves attractive to men. Men on the whole do not have to bother too much about their appearance to attract women; women are expected to look to them for other things. So women, on the whole, are looking for something other than sheer good looks in men; something which older men can supply.

That said, there is no doubt that older men remain attractive, or even become more attractive with a few character lines and hints of grey at the temples. There are plenty of the older generation of Hollywood stars – Cary Grant, Kirk Douglas, Paul Newman, who still played romantic leading roles into their sixties, while women of the same age are relegated to character parts. As Michelle Pfeiffer, who starred opposite Sean Connery in *The Russia House*, said: 'When I'm 62, are they going to let me play opposite a 32-year-old man, which was the age difference between me and Sean Connery in that film?'

Women film stars often find they have to dramatically change the kinds of roles they play once they enter their fifties, while male stars can go on playing the same kinds of roles for a decade or more. While female models' careers are often over by the time they reach their late twenties, male models can go on for far longer. This is because men are often viewed as being *more* attractive as they get older. Many women find older men more appealing physically than young, gawky males.

Petronella Wyatt, writing in the *Sunday Telegraph*, puts the attraction of an older man beautifully when she writes: 'The signs of ageing – those creases, wrinkles, grey hairs – are like the blue veins on a stilton, the things that give the cheese its piquant taste. An older man is brandy compared with apple juice, rich, dark chocolate as opposed to a Milky Bar.'

To marry a substantially older man is actually only to exaggerate something which is in the usual order of things. It is almost standard for women to marry men who are a little older than themselves. They want a man who is a little older in the same way that they want a man who is a little taller, a little stronger, than themselves; it emphasises the differences between them. Women may instinctively feel that they want their man to protect them; a man who is a little older, more mature, is more likely to be able to do that. As men get older, a decrease in physical strength may be made up for by wisdom and knowledge about how to do things. Many women who marry older men mention that they wanted – and found – security with them.

The other big attraction of older men is that they have usually advanced much further in their careers than younger men and thus more often have money – and with it, power. Older men can offer a more comfortable lifestyle. They can offer financial security, and they may already have such possessions as a big house and a powerful car which younger men, and couples, are struggling to obtain.

Older men can also often offer more emotional security. A man who already has a younger woman is much less likely to run off with another one. The older man may have had a lot of relationships and now be at a phase in his life when he wants to settle down with one woman. He may have learned through previous relationships much more about what women want and how to deal with them, and is often far more understanding.

Younger wives speak out

Jo, 40, married to Matthew, 58, puts this very well. 'I think what attracted me first was his reliability. I'd had lots of relationships with young men who were artists and musicians and they were so unreliable. I never knew where I was. If Matthew said he'd meet me at such-and-such a time and place, I knew he'd be there. I needed that, I found it made me feel good.'

Gillian, married to a man 15 years older, agrees. 'Why do I find older men attractive? Simply because they know themselves, they are not continually searching for what they want in life. They are settled and know what they are doing and have this maturity about them which is so much more attractive than some youthful character who has simply not settled down and is not quite sure what he wants from life.'

Since women generally mature earlier than men, women in their late teens and early twenties often find men – or boys – of the same age immature and irresponsible. Often the older man is in a position of power, wealth or influence compared with the woman and this in itself is attractive. There are many cases of secretaries marrying their bosses, actresses marrying their directors, students marrying their lecturers. Often these relationships begin with a kind of secrecy which further enhances them.

The experience of Christobel, a 30-year-old wardrobe consultant, illustrates all these points. She was 21 when she met her future husband, Gavin, who was then aged 37. She was one of his students. She said, 'When I met Gavin I didn't think of his age – I just fell in love. No, that's not quite true. But I just know a man of my own age wouldn't have appealed.

'He was very straight. He used to come to lectures in a pair of brown cords, a navy coat, and a navy scarf. I remember once I spent hours tying little bits of fluorescent fabric into the tassels of the scarf. It must have taken him hours to undo them. After I'd first been to his house and stayed the night we used to go in to college together and we'd get off the bus at different stops so we wouldn't arrive together. At college we would never meet or talk to one another. He was nervous that being involved with a student would be seen as professional misconduct.

'In many ways we were completely different, but I was always attracted to older men. I was attracted to my English teacher at school. When I was 15 I went out with a man who was 12 years older. I went out with men my own age too, but they had no depth, no experience. To live with someone I need these things.

'When I look at magazines I like older, rugged men, not the young, clean-shaven look. I like men with lined faces, I find older men sexy. I get on better with older men. When I'm working, if I'm on a shoot with an older man directing, I know I'm going to get on better.

'We lead quite independent lives. He doesn't tolerate parties of my young friends, though I get on with his older ones. We go out separately a lot – he babysits for me, I babysit for him. I like this; I see my friends with partners the same age and they do everything together. I think that's stifling. I don't feel I lose out –

I get the best of all worlds. I like having a percentage of my life separate.'

Older men have other attractions, too. They often have more confidence, more poise, and know how to handle women and make them feel attractive. Rachel, 33, met Howard, 61, at French evening classes. 'I found him very polite, well-mannered, courteous, gentlemanly.' For the first four months they went out together they called one another by their surnames, Mr. . . and Miss. . . 'We began our married life and were very happy together. I was inexperienced sexually. He was a gentle teacher and we enjoyed ourselves. He was proud of me and 'showed me off' to all his friends. He was very affectionate.'

Another younger wife recalls: 'I was attracted to Chris because he was courteous, gentlemanly, and made me feel special. He is kind and generous. Our opinions differ, but we don't argue. Chris is my intellectual superior in many ways but we learn a lot from one another.'

Marrying an older man can be a passport to sophistication; the older man can direct his younger wife in the ways of the world and offers the chance to enjoy more sophisticated activities.

Needs fulfilled

Psychiatrist Anthony Storr writes that nobody is ever completely whole, and therefore in all relationships there is an aspect of need. If that need is fulfilled by the other person, the couple can relate to one another as two whole people. Such relationships will be successful, even if to outsiders they may seem unusual.

Chris Clulow, chairman of the Tavistock Institute for Marital Studies, however, believes that marriages with a big age gap are likely to be 'mutually exploitative'. He says, 'For him it might represent a desperate clutching on to life, a fear of his potency running out, so he chooses someone with vitality and energy. For her, it can often be the sugar daddy, or mentor syndrome. He offers indulgence, security and attention – like being a favoured daughter.' But are not all marriages to some extent mutually exploitative? If it works, and both partners get what they need in the relationship, isn't everybody happy?

Marjorie, 38, married to Jim, 56, has a very happy marriage. 'We compliment one another in so many ways. I have always been insecure, emotionally up and down, and restless. All the young men I ever went out with couldn't cope with me – they said I was too demanding. What attracted me to Jim was that he was stable, sensible, and never let anything shake him. He was always the same. I knew exactly what he was like and that he wasn't going to change. That gave me enormous self-confidence.

'Because his first marriage broke up very painfully – his first wife left him for another man – I know he never wants to go through that again. He loves having a young and attractive wife, and our sex life is fantastic. I know he isn't going to run off with a younger woman because he's got a younger woman already! So I feel very secure with him, unlike some of my friends whose younger husbands are starting to look around at other women.'

Sometimes there is a clear inequality in a marriage, as where a young woman marries an older man who is held in high esteem for his achievements in life – especially the artist or 'genius'. Picasso had this appeal, and so did Charlie Chaplin. Chaplin had three ex-wives and a string of relationships behind him when he married Oona O'Neill, daughter of the playwright Eugene O'Neill, in 1943. The marriage was kept secret because her father disapproved. She was 18, Chaplin 54. By all accounts it was a very happy marriage. Their housekeeper, Mirella, is quoted as saying, 'I had never seen a couple so close, so much in love. They lived for each other right to the very end.'

The marriage lasted for 34 years. As Chaplin became increasingly frail, Oona remained devoted. Mirella recalls, 'When he became too weak to hold a fork she would feed him herself, patiently and lovingly. It was she who nursed him at the end. It was inspiring to see them together.'

The couple had eight children. After Chaplin died at the age of 88, Oona was devastated; she did not marry again.

Romantic overtones

The theme of the older man and the younger woman is one which recurs often in literature. Sometimes the portrait is drawn of a young, lively woman trapped in a relationship with an older, dried-up man, such as that of the marriage of Dorothea to Mr Causabon in George Eliot's *Middlemarch*. Dorothea, 'the elder of the sisters, was not yet 20.' She is lively, vivacious, attractive. Mr Causabon is 'A dried bookworm . . . he is over five and forty. I should say a good seven and twenty years older than you.'

The opposite picture is drawn in Jane Austen's *Sense and Sensibility* where Marianne, after a disastrous courtship with the dashing young Willoughby, finds happiness in marriage with the older and sensible Colonel Brandon, an 'absolute old bachelor' who is 'on the wrong side of five and thirty'. Marianne is 17 and points out that he is 'Old enough to be my father'. Even the sensible sister Elinor observes that 'Perhaps thirty-five and seventeen had better not have any thing to do with matrimony together'. However, such marriages were not uncommon among the wealthier sections of society, where marriages tended to be arranged, with wealth and position considered more important than love or other areas of compatibility.

Romantic fiction, too, often features a man who is older than the woman. Jane Eyre is only 18 when she meets her employer, the forbidding Mr Rochester. When he finally asks, 'Jane, will you marry me?' he describes himself as 'A crippled man, 20 years older than you, whom you will have to wait on'.

In much modern romantic fiction the woman falls for an older man. In fact, the man is almost invariably somewhat older than the heroine. Mills and Boon issue guidance for would-be authors which specifies that the book should concern true love between a woman aged 17-28 and a man aged 30-45 (must be rich and/or powerful). A great deal of popular romantic and escapist fiction concerns younger women in love with older men, often the nurse and famous surgeon, secretary and successful boss variety.

Real life prospects

Of course, such fantasies do come true in real life. Actor John Hurt was 48 when he met his second wife Jo Dalton, aged 30. One weekend, Hurt left the set without his script and Dalton was asked to take it to his flat. 'We met and had this incredible conversation,' she recalls. 'It was like we'd known one another forever.' She confesses she was frightened. 'I thought, it's too much like all those movies. Here's the leading actor and this girl who's working on her first film. I said to myself, this is splendid, romantic and mad, but is it going to come to any good?'

Women involved in such relationships obviously have fears about what kind of marriage they are going to make. People tend to choose partners from a similar social class and background and also age, with the idea that the more you have in common the more likely you are to get on successfully. But are these marriages any happier than those where there is a big age gap? Renate Olins, of the London Marriage Guidance Council, thinks that marriages to older men are not more likely to fail than any other marriages. 'In some ways, they may be more likely to succeed, because the couples are more likely to have put some thought into it. They are likely to have faced the questions of relatives and friends and to have thought about potential problems. Such marriages may be entered into with more pragmatism and less with rose-tinted glasses than marriages of a couple who seem ideally matched.'

Repeating a pattern

But what exactly is going on when a couple are attracted to one another? Dr Emmanuel Lewis of the Tavistock Institute for Marital Studies says that almost invariably the attraction is because, no matter how different the partners may appear on the surface, they each sense that the person they love has similar family background, problems and behaviour patterns as themselves, people who have shared similar experiences in childhood.

For example, a woman who marries an older man may do so because she is insecure and thinks that this older man may give her financial and emotional security. But it is likely that he may be insecure himself; hence the attraction for him of a younger woman who will make him seem more attractive to the outside world. Thus, a woman who had a weak father might marry a man who appears strong and dominant, but find on marrying him that this front covers his own weaknesses and fears, perhaps caused by the fact that he, too, had a weak father. It is surprising how often these patterns appear in marriages which go wrong.

Another example might be a woman who had an absent father who marries an older, more successful man only to find he, too, is absent all the time because he is so involved in running the business which made him so successful. Or the woman whose mother was widowed for 20 years who, perhaps unconsciously knowing she would repeat the pattern of her mother, marries an older man. Though such hidden motivations may be rare, they do exist.

Dr Lewis points out that the myth of Oedipus – often cited when talking about young men who have relationships with women old enough to be their mothers, or women with men old enough to be their fathers – actually illustrates how we tend to repeat patterns from the past. We may struggle to change these patterns, and may make a marriage thinking we are doing the opposite of our parents, only to find the same pattern emerging, just as in trying to destroy Oedipus his parents put in train the very string of events which led to the prediction they had feared.

However, there is a positive side to this, too. Couples sometimes achieve a much deeper understanding because they share the same fears. A sensible woman who realises that she missed out on a father might marry an older man and appreciate those qualities she missed – experience of the world, maturity, wisdom. If she is aware of this, it might work out well. Other women may accept that if they miss out on marriage in their twenties, the only men available might be older, divorced men, and accept that this kind of marriage is better than none at all. If people are aware of the reasons behind the choices they make, they are less likely to come across unexpected problems.

Some couples are aware of the risks and discuss them. 'When we first fell in love and started living together we talked a great deal about the age gap,' says Pippa, whose husband Paul is 21 years older. 'Paul said he wanted me to feel free to meet someone younger. But now we are used to it and other factors become more important. Paul's attitude to life is to grasp all opportunities with both hands and live life to the full. He has far more energy at 68 than some folk have in their twenties.'

Theresa and her husband, Martin, make a joke of it. 'Of course the age gap – 24 years – was important. He said it was all right when we married, at 35 and 59, but what about in 20 years time. We used to have a joke: just think, when you're 92, I'll be 116.'

Some of these age-gap marriages are entered into almost as a kind of business contract, knowing that they are unlikely to last. The older man might give the younger woman a step up the career ladder; she may then move on, rather as in *Pygmalion* Professor Higgins helps Eliza to move into new social circles and then inevitably loses her.

In pursuit

Another reason why women marry older men is the simple fact that often older men pursue them. The attraction of the younger woman for a man is obvious. Melvyn Bragg, in his book and screenplay *A Time to Dance*, shown on BBC television in early 1992, portrays a working-class girl of 18 who is attracted to and has an affair with a 55-year-old bank manager. The television mini-series caused a stir, partly because of the explicit sex scenes, but also because people were uncomfortable with the idea of such a big age gap.

For the man, such a relationship enables him to relive his youth, and restores his virility. The woman, too, may feel flattered at being pursued by somebody who is no mere schoolboy or student. In *A Time to Dance*, the girl, Bernadette, finds security and solace in the arms of the older man, making up for an episode of sexual abuse in the past. Presumably the older man's wisdom and sexual experience is supposed to help her here.

11

In this example, the middle-aged bank manager had an invalid wife. But one of the reasons why some men leave their middle-aged wives for a younger woman is that women who probably spent many years as wife and mother become more assertive and active once their children are older, refusing to live in the man's shadow any more. Often this coincides with a period in which the man is having doubts about his own role. Men who are unable to cope with this change may seek a still dependent and still adoring woman, who will almost inevitably be younger.

The stereotype of the older man and his adoring younger wife can be very irksome, though. Andrew is 41. He married his former secretary, Pauline, now aged 24, and they have a two-year-old son. He says, 'I do get some awful remarks, like you've got a real bimbo there, which is very unfair since Pauline is very intelligent. Some people say, you're a bit of a dirty old man, or call me her sugar daddy. But I'm not ashamed of it at all. I know Pauline looks fabulous. I won't pretend it's not a real ego boost to have a young lady like this on my arm who looks terrific. Yes, she makes me feel young; she makes me feel like a million dollars.'

Andrew feels that, important though it is, this is certainly not the most vital thing in their relationship. 'I think having a child has made a lot of difference. Having someone to look after is a real bond, it has brought us closer together.' (See Chapter 6.)

Getting to know one another

Often the attraction for an older man takes time to develop, perhaps unlike young love. Many younger women meet their older partners through work; this gives them time to get to know one another well before the relationship develops further. Brenda, now 38, met her husband Derek, 51, through work and then the local music society. She had been widowed at the age of 25, her first husband dying in a car accident and leaving her with a six-month-old baby. 'Derek was safe and secure; we were friends first, lovers second. Derek is a very youthful 50; when I was preparing for a party a neighbour asked, 'Is it the big 'O' then?' I said, 'Yes, he'll be 50.' And the neighbour said, '50! I meant 40. Surely he's only 40, isn't he?'

Brenda says the relationship is very different to that with her first husband, Paul. 'That was more romantic, passionate. But I don't live in the past; Derek and Paul are completely different. I think my experience at 25 matured me; people of my own age were too young for me. I'm not conscious of Derek being older than me. He's more conscious that I'm young. We joke about it, you know. He calls me his child bride and that kind of thing.'

Mary was 27 when she met her husband, David, aged 45, at work. 'I didn't find him particularly attractive at first,' she says. 'I liked him, we got on well, but I think partly because I knew he was married I didn't think of him in a romantic light. Then as we got to know one another better I think I became aware of an attraction, but didn't give it much thought because I thought he was happily married. It was only when I came to leave the job that I suddenly realised I couldn't bear not to see him again.'

Margaret, 38, whose husband is 56, denies that there was any special attraction in an older man. 'I fell in love with Tim and that was that,' she says. 'I would have fallen in love with him whatever his age. I didn't consciously choose to marry an older man. I was aware of the dangers. But how can you turn your back on something like this? Was I to say, because he might die young, or because we might have problems later on, I should turn my back on love, children, and happiness which might last 10 or 20 years in the hope that I might meet a man my age? Supposing I never did?'

Margaret also feels that for women in their thirties, an older man may be the only choice. 'Quite a few of my friends my own age are not married,' she says. 'Most of my friends who did marry did so in their twenties. By the time you reach your thirties you realise that all the men are married, except those who are gay or odd in some way. So that leaves you only with older men whose first marriages are in trouble. In many ways you don't have the choice of a man your own age.'

Gold diggers and marriage breakers

How do other people view the marriages of younger women and older men? Beliza Ann Furman, of the American organisation WOOM, Wives Of Older Men, says that younger wives usually suffer from two stereotype images: the gold digger, and the marriage breaker. Many people assume the young woman marries an older man only for his money or position. Or they assume that she has stolen someone else's husband.

Of course, some women do marry an older man for his money or power. Some women feel that an older man is special or powerful, but they haven't seen the process by which he got there. Some first wives lose out, having made all the sacrifices that enabled their husband to make it rich, they then see a younger woman walk off with the spoils. But in most marriages, there is much more to it than that.

Because Gail's husband was wealthy, everyone – including her own family – assumed that she was marrying him for the money. 'I really resented this,' says Gail. 'Of course, I wouldn't have married anyone who was unemployed or had no prospects. But the money is a plus, it wasn't the main attraction. They said, you're only 25, he's very good-looking at 40, but wait 20 years and see what happens. What do I want to wait 20 years for? I'm happy now.'

The second accusation often made against younger wives, that they were responsible for the break-up of the first marriage, is a more complicated issue. Often the husband does leave his first wife for the younger woman. However, very few men will leave a happy marriage and go through all the trauma of divorce, especially when there are children, just to be with a younger woman. Often the marriage is unhappy and the appearance of the other woman brings out into the light of day what was pushed under the carpet.

Brenda's husband Derek was still married when she met him. She says, 'I think I was the catalyst rather than the cause of the marriage break-up. They had had problems for many years. David and his ex had agreed that they shouldn't be together. His ex was very accepting of this at first; but when she actually realised he would leave her for me she was upset.'

For Mary and David the situation was very similar. 'I knew he was married, so I didn't make any moves towards him. I think I switched off from the attraction because I didn't want to have an affair. Then he told me that he was desperately unhappy in his marriage, that his wife had been having an affair, and that he had been considering leaving her. She would have left him had her lover been available. Of course, what everybody saw was that he left his wife for me.'

In fact, Frances Pyne of the Dateline agency says that very few women do set out to find a man who is much older than themselves. She feels that where there is a big age gap people have less in common – they miss out in particular on shared memories. Many more relationships between older men and younger women begin in the workplace or develop out of friendship than are 'love at first sight'.

Chapter 2

THE FATHER FIGURE?

'I often find that a woman whose father was a remote authoritarian figure may look for an older man who resembles her father, yet is warm and affectionate and gives her approval. It's a way of sorting out the "unfinished business" that every daughter has with her father.'

RENATE OLINS
of the London Marriage Guidance Council

When people debate the reasons why women marry older men, the first thing they are likely to think of is that they are marrying a father figure. The cliché, 'He's old enough to be your father,' gives this thought away. Similarly, when people look at the reasons for a man marrying a younger woman, they are likely to think of it in terms of the Lolita syndrome. (In Nabokov's famous novel, middle-aged Humbert Humbert is perversely attracted to pubescent girls, in particular 12-year-old Lolita).

The idea of marrying a father figure may, of course, explain some such marriages. Renate Olins of the London Marriage Guidance Council says some women look for someone who can replace their father. 'For example,' she says, 'I often find that a woman whose father was a remote authoritarian figure may look for an older man who resembles her father, yet is warm and

17

affectionate and gives her approval. It's a way of sorting out the "unfinished business" that every daughter has with her father.' If the marriage does not work out, the woman may go on trying to replace him through a succession of marriages.

What is the 'unfinished business' that daughters have with their fathers? According to Freud, a young girl of three to six has powerful sexual feelings which she projects on her father, often behaving as if she were 'in love' with him. The daughter would like to have her father to herself and feels aggressively towards her mother, even fantasising that she would like to get rid of her. This 'Electra Complex' is the reverse of the famous Oedipus Complex. In a healthy family relationship, the father will 'flirt' with his daughter, cuddle her and show her that he loves her and finds her attractive, but will not make any overt sexual moves towards her because of the very powerful incest taboo. When the girl emerges from the period of sexual latency, which lasts from seven to puberty, she will feel confident in her sexuality and begin to look at other men.

If the father, however, is absent or cold, or makes it plain that he disapproves of his daughter or her behaviour, she may seek this kind of relationship with an older man in the way that Renate Olins suggests. If her father goes too far in the other direction and breaks the incest taboo, she will have great difficulties in forming satisfying sexual relations or a happy marriage later on.

Destiny

Of course, saying that a woman is seeking a father figure is far too simplistic in most cases. On the whole, people marry for much more complex and often hidden reasons. Sometimes the desire to marry an older man seems rooted deep in childhood – destiny at work. Like the myth of Oedipus (in which the boy is put out to die on the hillside because his parents are told he will kill his father and marry his mother – and he not only survives but fulfils the prophecy), it sometimes seems as if we end up doing what, consciously, we may have been trying to avoid.

There was a big age gap between Marjorie's maternal grand-parents; her grandfather was over 10 years older than her grandmother. Marjorie's mother always said how happy they were, but when Marjorie, in her teens, said she found an older friend of the family attractive, her mother gave her a solemn lecture on how you should never marry anyone more than 10 years older. 'I remember at the time being puzzled and thinking, why is she telling me this? I have no intention of doing any such thing.'

Yet, in her mid twenties, Marjorie had to break the news to her mother that she was going to marry a divorced man who was nearly 20 years older than herself. Before she could get the words out, her mother said, 'I know what you're going to tell me; it's an older man.' Marjorie was stunned. She could not imagine how her mother had known.

There was also a big age gap between Brenda's parents, something which had always worried her. 'My mother was 15 years younger than my father. Most of my teenage years I vowed I would never make the same mistake.' Yet some years later she married a man nearly 14 years older than herself.

Another woman recalled having a tarot reading done when she was about 20. 'I remember that it showed an older man who would dominate my life,' she says. 'At the time I dismissed it as nonsense. Yet, 10 years later, here I am married to a man who is 25 years older than myself.'

Ellen, now married to a man 18 years older, had always been attracted to older men. 'I remember when I was a teenager I would always end up at parties talking to the only older men who were around. I was the kind of girl who would discuss God with the vicar or science with a friend of my father's who was a physicist rather than dance with boys of my own age. At university I befriended a much older lecturer – this was an absolutely platonic relationship – and later I acted as a kind of secretary to a man in his eighties who had moved in literary circles between the wars and had fascinating anecdotes to tell. My friends used to call them "Ellen's older men".'

When there is an age gap of 10-15 years people are more likely to be accepting and put it down to love than where there is a really big gap of 20-30 years or more. Here something far more shocking seems to be at work; it is as if people cannot help but see something incestuous in such liaisons. When Jacqueline, in her twenties, ran off with her brother's tutor at university (he was almost 70), her father refused to have him in the house or to recognise the marriage.

Lesley married a man 30 years her senior when she was 32 and they now have a small son. People's reactions to the marriage were very mixed, she says. 'A lot of people I knew, while saying nice things on the surface, were obviously worried by it. When I announced that I was pregnant they were rather amazed and disconcerted. When we are out, a lot of people refer to Jim as my father or to me as his daughter. Depending on the situation, we either put them right or just carry on as if they hadn't said anything. It gets very boring explaining to everyone'.

Sometimes people play up to this confusion. 'I took my husband to the hospital when he was going in for an operation and we had to report to Admissions. The woman at the desk said, "Could you and your father wait over there". I didn't put her right, but we went and sat by the window and started kissing one another in an obviously sexual way. I don't know what she thought; we rather enjoyed the laugh.'

Sometimes couples play up to the father/daughter role, at least in public, because it seems to be expected of them. 'There's something vaguely naughty about it; and I enjoy it,' says Rosamund, whose partner is 25 years her senior. 'I love the fact that he is older, wrinkly, slightly seedy; I don't know why, it turns me on. It turns me on that other people disapprove of us and look at us in the street; when we walk along holding hands or kiss at a bus-stop I see people looking at us and wondering what's going on. I suppose they think this is an illicit affair, not a marriage of 10 years standing.'

Denial

Some women deny that there is any element of a father-figure involved. Christobel's husband is 15 years older. 'Although my parents divorced and my father didn't live with us from the time I was nine, I absolutely refute that I am looking for a father-figure. I saw my father regularly, I get on well with him. People think the kind of woman who marries an older man wants to be looked after, coddled, coaxed through life, have decisions made for her – that's not me. But I need emotional support. Young men just can't give it. They say, "Oh, I'm not ready for that".'

Some men, too, dismiss the 'father figure' idea. 'There is nothing of a father-daughter relationship between me and Carol,' says Derek, who, at 50, is 22 years older than his wife. 'Even though Carol is the same age as my children, I never think of her in a fatherly way. Anyway, the idea is ridiculous . . . if I behaved towards my daughters as I do to Carol I'd be arrested!'

Anthony Storr, the psychiatrist, writes that there are obviously people who are seeking a parent in their heterosexual partner. But, he says, people who do so can hardly be said to be falling in love in the full sense, and a study of their psychology invariably reveals the presence of sexual fantasies which have little to do with their partner. 'A woman who has married a kind and elderly man, to whom she is really a daughter, will tend to have fantasies of a ruthless and powerful young lover who is perpetually engaged in abducting her to some romantic destination.'

Rosamund laughs at this idea; 'All my sexual fantasies are perfectly fulfilled by Gerald. We are passionate about one another.' Rosamund denies that she is looking for a father figure; 'I have a perfectly good relationship with my father and we are fond of one another. I have a father; I wasn't looking for another one.'

Oona Chaplin, 36 years younger than her husband, said: 'People seem to think of Charlie as my father, but age counts for nothing in this house. To me he seems younger every day. There is certainly no father fixation about my feelings for him. He has made me mature and I keep him young.'

When Jacqueline Kennedy married Aristotle Onassis in October 1968, there was a public outcry and much speculation on her motives. One newspaper columnist wrote that it was the marriage of one of the world's most expensive women to one of the world's richest men. The age difference was 23 years; she was

39, he was 62. One psychiatrist was quoted as saying that she was seeking a 'grandfather figure.' Since Jackie's sister had also married a man 20 years her senior, there was speculation that the two sisters' relationship with their father might account for their predilection for older men.

There seems little doubt that the marriage was not one of love and that it deteriorated with time. There was a complicated marriage contract with over 200 clauses, and when Onassis died after some weeks of illness it was his daughter who was at his bedside – Jackie was in New York.

Husbands as parents

Jenny talks very honestly about her feelings for her husband who was 20 years older than herself. 'Sid was the principal of the college where I worked. I suppose that made him a father figure in itself. He was well respected and looked after the staff. I don't think I was particularly attracted to older men; I had fallen for two older men when I was a schoolgirl, both teachers, but since then had only been attracted to men of my own age.

'My first reaction was that I didn't want anything to develop because of the difference in age. I felt there would be tensions between what he wanted to do and what I wanted. I wanted to go out more. In fact, when he was my age I know he went out all the time, but he had changed. I felt this could be a restriction.

'I was also reluctant because of the way I thought it would appear to the world – she's unattractive, she can't do any better. And then the knowledge that he would grow old and die before me.

'I feel that in many ways Sid parented me and that was important because I had not been adequately parented. My parents divorced when I was very young and I was brought up by my mother and my grandmother; I used to see my father only on visits. When I was six my father delivered me to boarding school and I remember feeling utterly abandoned when he left me there, although I still saw him regularly over the years. Obviously I missed out on a more normal father/daughter relationship.

'Sid contributed enormously to my having the kind of confidence parents would normally give their children. I relied on his great dependability – he was a very rock-like figure, and I feel I've internalised some of that attitude.

'I am going to tell you a dream that I had because I think it is significant.

'Before I married Sid I dreamt that I saw a man at Notting Hill tube station. This was where Sid worked and where my father had lived. This man either was my father and resembled Sid or vice versa. I think it's significant that even very soon after the dream I couldn't remember which way round it was.'

After five years of marriage, Sid died from cancer. Jenny says 'I would much rather be this age and widowed than unmarried. I am on a secure financial footing; I'm provided for by Sid as well as having my own earning power.'

Act of regression

Many women who marry older men and allow these men to dominate them, may also be marrying a father figure, even if they won't admit it. They may be regressing to the stage in childhood where they could blame their wicked father for everything.

Eve's marriage was like this. Her husband was a man 25 years her senior, and she had to defer to him in everything. She was unable to go out, meet people or take part in any activities outside the house without asking his permission, which was frequently not granted. She had to have everything in the house organised to his satisfaction and arranged around his routines. She blamed his presence for the fact that she was unable to have any other close relationships or friendships and could not take a job.

In other marriages, the situation is rather reversed, with the man doing everything to placate his younger wife and make sure she has no cause to leave him, showering her with gifts, allowing her any licence, even allowing her to go out with or make love to other men rather than leave him. Often, however, the younger wife loses respect for the husband and the marriage falls apart.

Sometimes the younger wife, while she is still young, plays the role of the little girl or the flirtatious teenager. However, as she matures this becomes less appropriate and marital problems can develop when the wife starts to grow up and want a more equal kind of relationship.

Husband's four roles

Eva Loewe, a Jungian analyst who has considered this subject in depth, suspects that the marriage to an older man is an archetypal image which possibly all women fantasise about, to such an extent that she wonders if it's a dream which is thwarted when a woman marries a man her own age. She points out that in any marriage the husband has four roles: lover, brother, father and mentor. In the marriage of a younger woman to an older man, the elements of father and mentor are likely to be most prominent.

In the early years of the marriage, the man is likely to fulfil most of these functions adequately. However, as he ages, there may be problems. For many years one woman lived with a man 25 years her senior. 'I thought it would only last 10 years. I had a child from a former relationship and then we had twins together. As 15, then 20 years passed, I realised that I felt he ought to have died. He was too old; I wanted to be more active sexually.'

Fantasy element

Women married to older men often suffer from extreme guilt in ending the relationship. A woman is attracted to an older man, finds him endearing, and later realises that the same qualities make it hard for her to leave him. This may stem from the fantasies at work when a woman marries an older man. 'I felt I would be the one who, against all the predictions to the contrary, would not tire of him or betray him.' Then you have to face up to the possibilities that the outside world may have been right.

This may make things doubly difficult if problems develop in the relationship. Instead of being the rock the woman leans on, the older man becomes a weak, defenceless, pathetic figure, with all his charisma and powers gone, and nothing before him but a lonely and bitter old age if his wife leaves him for another.

In some marriages of younger women to older men there is the fantasy of 'making good.' Marianne puts this well when she says, 'My husband, who is 18 years older, had had a very unhappy and sexually unfulfilled first marriage. When I met him I thought, I can make up to him for this bad experience, I can show him what love is.' The older man, suitably grateful for the woman who has healed the wounds of the past and restored his youth, adores the younger wife with an intensity which makes it doubly hard for her to leave him later on. Indeed, part of the attraction of the older man is that he bestows on his young wife the adoration in which she can bask. And he feels he has a special prize for which he is grateful.

Sometimes this feeling of the preciousness of the younger wife leads to an unhealthy situation where the man controls the woman through money – she becomes the bird in the golden cage. He buys things for her, keeps her in luxury, yet makes sure she does not have the money in her own hands which would give her freedom and the possibility of escape. This pattern may be at work in marriages where the wife complains that her older husband is tight with money – a tightness which she may blame on being brought up in a different generation but which is likely to have a more deep-rooted cause.

Where there is an age difference, the man is more likely to have more money and want to control his wife through money. Conflicts about how to spend money are usually power struggles; after all, the issue is not who has the money but who decides how it is spent.

Martha, in her 30s, says money was never a problem when she was earning, because she could always buy what she really wanted. 'Once I stopped working, to have a child, I was totally dependent,' she says. 'I had to ask him for every little thing and he used to really humiliate me by making me have to ask repeatedly for a small sum of money he had said I could have, or sometimes refuse it altogether.'

Eva Loewe says that women who are uncertain about themselves are often attracted to the security an older man gives. Such a woman is likely to say: 'I was sure of him emotionally because he was older and less likely to look at another woman. I couldn't bear to go again through the betrayal I had experienced with a younger man.'

Other women admit that they are trying to escape the pattern of their parents' unhappy marriage. 'My mother did not respect my father and constantly undermined him, criticising him and mocking him in our eyes . . . I resented the fact that he did not stand up to her. I wanted to marry a man I could respect. I married an older man who was looked up to within his profession, somebody who I would not be able to mock and who the children, too, would be respectful of.'

Sexual archetypes

The pairing of an older man with a younger woman has a certain charm about it: the attraction of opposites; winter and spring.

Eva Loewe believes that the Jungian archetype of the Magus, the magician, and his younger female apprentice together tending the alchemic cauldron fits many age-gap marriages. There are incestuous overtones but the desire for incest is transformed in the relationship between mentor and accomplice into the creativity of alchemy.

Some younger women and older men speak of the frisson they get from incestuous overtones. 'I'm not going to deny it; I know it's there and I enjoy it,' says David, whose wife Joanna is 20 years younger. His wife agrees. 'I think every woman must have deep-seated fantasies about being with their father and I suppose you can carry these further if your lover is much older.' Joanna enjoyed her seduction of David; other women, too, feel that it is easy to seduce an older man, much as they were able to get adoration from their father on his knee. This fits in with the Biblical story of Lot who was made drunk by his daughters and lured into sleeping with one of them.

Another archetype which is at work in some age-gap marriages is that of Joseph and Mary, the older man who does not have sex with his young wife and who even understands that she has conceived by another. It is expected of Mary to be pure and the older man does not want to debauch her. Some older men are not very sexually active with a young wife and may even let her feel that she can take a lover. (See also Chapter 7.)

'He led me to believe that he would understand if I took a lover,' says Vivienne, who had an affair when she was 40 and her husband 64. 'By that time, I think I had come to see him in a more paternal role and sex wasn't what was important in our marriage. Of course, when he actually was confronted by this he was deeply wounded and told me he had never intended this at all. He had always expressed his fears that I would not be satisfied by him and that a younger man could satisfy me better, which made my "betrayal" of him seem even more painful, I think, than if he had been the same age as me.'

Long-term prospects

The younger woman who marries an older man and then finds herself revolted by him as he ages may well have experienced a poor relationship with her father, says Eva Loewe. Again, she believes this is a variant of the Joseph-Mary kind of marriage; the older man believes he should respect his wife and not touch her sexually.

There may be a dependency too in such marriages, where the younger wife believes that her older husband – like her father – will pay for her, support her, and take care of her. The younger wife can always turn to the older husband for financial and emotional support. However, when the man gets older this situation may be reversed. The younger wife may actually need to earn money when the man is retired and take over responsibility for many things. Eva Loewe believes that, for this reason, many women who marry older men are attracted to more difficulties but also seek to learn and overcome them. A woman who marries an older man knows she is likely to have a harder journey and may end up alone later in her life. (See Chapter 8).

Because of this she will have to learn from the older partner and take on many of his roles. Women who marry an older man are often empowered by him to develop confidence and skills which can lead to greater fulfillment and independence when she is on her own again, as Jenny said of Sid. (See pages 22-3.) The wife of an older man may become stronger, more capable and more independent later on, having taken into herself the qualities for which she admired and loved her husband.

Chapter 3

THE EARLY YEARS OF MARRIAGE

For better for worse, for richer for poorer, in sickness and in health.

BOOK OF COMMON PRAYER

§ Most people expect to be happy at least at the outset of their marriage. Even those who have doubts about the wisdom of marrying older men expect most of these marriages to start off happy, or, at least, with the woman getting what she wants in terms of financial status and security. Fortunately, many such marriages *are* very successful – as we'll see later in this chapter.

However, as we have already seen, sometimes there can be problems with such a marriage from the outset. Beliza Ann Furman of the American organisation WOOM, Wives of Older Men, says that there are three main concerns faced by women who marry older men. There is prejudice against a woman who may be viewed as a gold-digger or marriage-breaker, isolation because she does not fit in with other couples of her generation, and the problem of bridging the generation gap – of understanding the different ways in which the couple were brought up.

Family opposition

Many women who marry older men also meet opposition from their families. 'In the early days parental opposition was extremely fierce,' writes Anita, whose husband was 44 when she married him aged 25. 'My mother did everything she could to destroy the friendship, by both fair means and very foul. In fact I had twelve months of sheer hell. No one thought we would stick it and I think Jack had his doubts about how I could cope at times.'

'At my father's request we waited 12 months to get married. But the atmosphere at home was so terrible after six months that he himself suggested I brought the date forward. I think my father had hoped that by the delay I would change my mind.'

While some parents are upset when a marriage to an older man is announced, they usually come round in time. Jenny, who married 26-years-older Brian, recalls, 'At first my mother burst into tears and my father said he wouldn't have him in the house. When it came to the wedding they did attend, though they weren't very happy about it. But they gradually came to like Brian. By the time I had my first child – their first grandchild – they had totally accepted him, and were over the moon about the baby.'

Reactions of the family of the husband to a second marriage can also be difficult. 'My husband's family just wouldn't accept me for years,' says Susan, whose husband has two teenage children by his first marriage. 'They kept referring to Jan, his first wife, as part of "the family" and wanted to invite her to all the family occasions and to stay with the children, in addition to the occasions when we took the children to stay. They found it very difficult to introduce me to people as Tim's wife – they once or twice actually did introduce me as Tim's "new" or "second" wife. They were always talking about her in front of me. They still had her and Tim's wedding photo on the mantelpiece until I actually asked Tim to explain how it upset me and ask them to remove it.'

If either partner's parents are opposed to the marriage, it is best to try to discuss the matter with them and find out what their reservations are so that these can be dealt with if possible. If they remain unconvinced – even hostile – try not to get too upset. Usually they will come round in time when they see how happy you are together, especially if there are grandchildren.

When friends create problems

With friends it may be more difficult, because you can lose friends far more easily than you can lose family. Jenny says, 'A lot of my friends reacted badly. One actually said, "It's all right now, but what will you do when he's senile?" Others obviously couldn't understand what I saw in him. They would say things like "I couldn't see myself going to bed with an older man . . ." People were not very considerate of my feelings.

'John doesn't get on with some of my friends either. They are all much younger and into very different things. When I get together with girlfriends he just groans and goes out. I'm sure they think he is a terrible fuddy-duddy although he isn't at all.

'I don't exactly hit it off with *his* friends – I suppose because they are much older than I am. They all knew John with his first wife, Cath, and they had all done things together. His friends' wives were all jealous of me at first, because I was young and they were all insecure and afraid that their husbands would do the same thing, although this was very unfair as it was Cath's decision to end the marriage.'

Being open about the age gap and making a joke of it can help defuse awkward situations. 'I had to introduce Derek to an old friend who was visiting us,' remembers Caroline. 'My friend knew he was 60 and I don't know what she expected. Derek was out when she arrived and we were having tea when I heard him come in. "Come and meet Anne," I called out, "Have you got your zimmer frame?" In bounded this incredibly lithe, handsome, healthy man. I think she realised the absurdity of her expectations because she laughed out loud.'

Dealing with friends who don't understand can be upsetting and, in the long term, may not be worth the effort. It can help to accept philosophically that you'll drift away from some friends; but you will probably make new ones as a couple. 'We did lose touch with quite a few of my old friends,' recalls Marjorie. 'I was in a very lively circle of musicians and artists who all used to drop round on one another. Jim didn't fit into that at all, so when we married a lot of my friends thought I'd just opted out and we didn't see that much of one another any more.'

It is important that neither partner is expected to relinquish all their old friendships, however. Both should be prepared to make some effort to accommodate one another's allies. To do otherwise only leads to resentment or even bitterness and a gradual erosion of the marriage.

When there is a large age gap, couples sometimes face difficulties because people do not believe they are married. 'I was a young-looking 35 and Henry was getting on for 60, grey-haired and looked his age. When we booked into hotels people obviously thought that I was not his wife and that we were having a dirty weekend. We joked about this, I probably even enjoyed it at first, but now I find it a bit of a bore.'

Gillian recalls, 'One of the women who worked at the factory where we met decided that I needed to be "warned" against what she seemed to regard as this "older philandering man". Other people didn't know how to react . . . even now I see funny little looks of surprise on the faces of people who realise this is my *husband*, not my *father!*'

Emerging differences

The 'generation gap' may not seem important when a couple are first in love but emerges soon enough when they settle down to living together. 'There are nearly 20 years between us; enough for Tim to have been my father,' says Ellen, 32. 'I notice that there are things he does differently. For instance, when I compare him to my friends' husbands who are the same age as me, they have quite different attitudes. They are more into sharing family responsibilities and looking after the children; they are less sexist. From time to time Tim comes out with things that I feel my father might have said and that really brings me up short, because I never saw him in that light at all initially.'

Attitudes to money

Sometimes the differences in life experiences can cause problems. 'Robert is very mean,' says Sally, who is 16 years younger than her husband. 'He was a child during the war and he is always making things go further, not wasting things. He goes around the house turning lights off and the heating down and I go around turning them back on and up again. He says he's being modern and ecological but actually I feel it's much more deep-seated than that. I suppose he is thinking of his retirement and making provision for that, while I'm thinking about having a good time while we're still young enough to enjoy ourselves.'

In these situations it may be that the man feels insecure and is using money as a way of controlling his wife's behaviour. She may be able to help by making her own financial contribution to the marriage, or by reassuring him that he is not in any danger of her leaving him, even if she wishes to go off on her own sometimes.

Marjorie, too, finds her husband is lacking in enthusiasm for new ventures. 'Whenever I suggest anything, he's always done it all, seen it all. He lived and travelled abroad a lot with his first family, living in Switzerland and France and working for international organisations. I would like to do that now but we can't. To begin with, he's too old to get another job; he feels he's stuck where he is now till he retires.'

Obviously, more give and take is needed in relationships where the couple start off with very different expectations. 'One problem we come across is that I am hungry for new experiences and he's not,' says Jo, who is 18 years younger than Matthew. 'For example, we had the opportunity to do a swap with a colleague of my husband's in New York and spend a year there. I really wanted to go, but Matthew didn't. He said he couldn't face the upheaval. Then I found out he'd done a very similar thing about 20 years ago, when he was still married to his first wife. That made me furious; I felt I'd missed out.'

It is certainly true that unless a man is at the top of his career in middle age he is likely to have far fewer career options than a younger man, who may change his job every few years, moving up the career ladder, while the older man may have to stay put. Marjorie feels this is reflected in other areas of life. 'He often says, I can't be bothered. When we were going through a bad patch, I asked him if he'd consider having an affair and his reply was, "I couldn't be bothered". I found that insulting; I want him to stay with me because he wants to, not because he can't be bothered to look for anyone better.'

In any marriage, people's interests may differ, but this seems to matter most when there is a big age gap. 'I found that we had less and less in common with one another,' says Christine. 'I know I look round at other friends' marriages and they don't have interests in common either, but they do at least have the same experiences to talk about. They were at university at the same time, they listened to the same songs at the same stage in their life. Things were very different when I was a student in the early seventies from when Jeff was a student in the fifties.'

Attitudes to sex

Attitudes to sex in particular have changed, and this can affect many marriages. 'I feel sorry for Jeff and his ex-wife,' says Christine, 38; Jeff is 56. 'In the fifties, when he got married the first time, he was very inexperienced sexually. People weren't sexually liberated in the way that we take for granted today. When he first had an affair with me he was completely swept off his feet; he said he didn't know sex could be like this.

'But it caused problems, too. It wasn't just that I did these things because I loved him, although I did, but that he realised I'd done them with other boyfriends; and, of course, I'd had a lot more boyfriends that he'd had girlfriends. Sex was much more important to him than it was to me.'

Where there is a big generation gap it's likely that the younger partner will have had a richer and more varied sex life than the older one, though this isn't always the case. At the beginning of a relationship, the man is likely to be very interested in sex. There is the excitement of the new relationship, the turn-on of having a younger woman in bed with him, and often a more exciting sexual experience that he's had before. But this can wear off, setting up problems and causing the younger woman to have fears about the future.

Sometimes friends or acquaintances will warn a younger wife that her husband might, when she ages, look for a still younger wife. This is paradoxical when, often, one of the motivations for marrying an older man is security – and the fact that the husband is less likely to leave. 'I think people saw me as a kind of bimbo,' says one younger wife. 'People said, "Remember, there's always someone younger and better-looking than you out there".' That could, of course, be said to either partner – so don't let it phase you.

Right about everything

One tendency that Carol noticed is that the older man tends to think that because of his age he is the boss. 'Because Derek is 22 years older than me he says things like, "When you've been around for as long as I have you'll realise . . ." and "I tried it like that once and it didn't work" and that kind of thing. It can be very difficult persuading him that I might be right about something. Of course, all men like to be right about everything, but I think with an older man this is exaggerated.' Derek, aged 50, seems to confirm this. 'The age gap only matters because of the difference in our experiences. I give her advice but she ignores me completely.'

Quality of relationship

Many marriages to an older man start off by being very happy. Jenny writes: 'I am 46. Four years ago when I met the man to whom I'm now married, he was nearly 64! It is an extraordinary love story. A common belief is that women marry older men for their money, but this is not true in our case – he had (and has) none. I think it's the quality of the relationship that counts, despite the age gap. We have a lot of fun together. We laugh a lot and love a lot. He has enormous energy and drive, more than my first husband had in his twenties.'

Many women married to older men talk of the quality of their relationship, and how, perhaps because they are aware that their time might be shorter, they tend to live more fully than those in more conventional relationships. This attitude is particularly strong when both partners are older, as expressed very clearly by Anne-Marie, who married Geoffrey when she was 44 and he 65. 'We're so aware that we both could have continued on our own or in empty marriages, instead of which we have found this tremendous happiness and fulfillment with one another. Every day I wake up and think: I am so lucky, she says. 'But Geoffrey has had a heart attack – though he's perfectly healthy now – and so I'm aware that we might only have one, five, ten years together. So we want to enjoy life now and not waste our time rowing over silly things and having pointless disagreements.'

The same point was made by Sandy, 53, married to philosopher-scientist James Lovelock, 72, in an interview she gave to the *Independent on Sunday*. 'When you're in your twenties you have your entire life ahead of you, but when you fall in love at our age you take each day as it comes and are grateful for it.' He says, 'The age disparity worried me, but when you're sure of each other it makes no difference. We're so delighted in each other's company we want none other.'

Ruth also found happiness with her second, older husband after an experience of an unhappy marriage to a man her own age. 'I was 50 and my husband 64 when we married just over two years ago. He was a widower who had been finally released from an unhappy marriage. He was as bruised and vulnerable as I was, being a "big softie" and yet having been starved for years of emotional and physical love. The chemistry was right – and still is! What he lacks in stamina he makes up for in desire.

'Obviously there are always fears that you and your older partner will not have long together, that he may become ill and die, but my brother-in-law died unexpectedly at the early age of 36 and my partner's mother celebrated her 100th birthday. I decided there are no guarantees and went for quality. (See also Chapters 7 and 8.)

'Most of the time I must admit I like having an "older man" for a husband because he makes me feel young. He is a big strong man and I sometimes have difficulty keeping up with him!'

Anne has lived with her former boss, who is 29 years older than her, for three years. She borrows a term from computer technology – WYSIWYG (what you see is what you get) – to describe his honesty and lack of pretence. 'He was set in his ways and I loved the security of knowing that what I saw was what I got,' she says. 'He's full of life and not at all self-centred. And a man that age knows how to please a woman.'

Happiness can be found even in the most unlikely situations. 'My husband developed rheumatoid arthritis soon after we married, when I was 22 and he was 37, and I guess some people, just judging him by appearances, would have considered him to be even older than he looks. Because Graham is crippled with arthritis now you might think it isn't much of a life or marriage but you couldn't be more wrong. Graham is totally the world's best husband and father. His only fault lies in worrying too much about me and the children. His caring, loving attitude is beyond comparison to anyone.'

The right attitude

Happiness is far more likely when a woman has realistic expectations of her marriage, much more likely to sour when the truth is not faced. Jennifer married Richard when she was 24 and he was 40. She says, 'Richard is incredibly youthful looking. I don't think anyone would know he is that much older than me. We never think about our ages; it's just not relevant to us.' Asked how she thought she would feel when she was 44 and he was 60, she considered for a moment and then said, 'I can't see that far ahead. We love one another, why shouldn't things work out?'

Marion has put much more thought into her situation. She is 36, her husband 55, and they have two young children. 'We agreed that he would work and support me while the children are young and that when he retires I'll be the main wage-earner,' she says. 'I'm continuing to work part-time – just two days a week – so that I don't lose out too much on my career and it won't be so difficult to get back into things.' (See also Chapter 7.)

Lucy, married to a man 16 years older, is sure there will be difficulties. 'I don't think you can fool yourself into thinking that there won't be problems,' she says. 'But then, every relationship has its problems. I really believe that marriage is a commitment and you have to see it through. We've chosen to marry one another, we have to make sure we do our best to make it work out.'

Chapter 4

SEX AND
THE OLDER MAN

On thy wither'd lips and dry,
Which like barren furrows lye,
Brooding kisses I will pour,
Shall thy youthful Heart restore.
Such kind Show'rs in Autumn fall,
And a second Spring recall:
Nor from thee will ever part,
Ancient Person of my Heart.

Thy Nobler Part(s), which but to name,
In our Sex wou'd be counted shame,
By Age's frozen grasp possest,
From their Ice shall be releast;
And, soothed by my reviving Hand,
In former Warmth and Vigor stand.
All a Lover's Wish can reach,
For thy Joy my Love shall teach:
And for thy pleasure shall improve,
All that Art can add to Love.
Yet still I love thee without Art,
Ancient Person of my Heart.

JOHN WILMOT, EARL OF ROCHESTER
*A Song of a Young Lady
to her Ancient Lover*

Sexual attraction forms the basis of most marriages and those to older men are no exception. However, in a society which places physical attractiveness above all else – and equates sexuality with youth – people wonder not only why women find older men attractive, but about their sexual relationship.

Those women who talk about their sexual relationship with older men are on the whole positive. One woman said, 'As for sex – grab yourself an older man, girls!' Another said, 'Having been married to both a man my age and then to an older man, all I can say is that sex was far better the second time around. I think an older man is less concerned with his own pleasure and more concerned with yours – or rather, he takes pleasure in giving you pleasure. My first husband used to make love quickly, roll over and go to sleep; my second husband and I can make love for hours.'

There is no denying that ageing does affect men's sexual response. In some ways, this is an advantage for women – especially the fact that it takes an older man longer to reach orgasm, thus prolonging the sexual act to the woman's advantage. But what are the changes which take place as a man ages? How long can he continue to satisfy his wife sexually?

Medical research, such as that carried out by Masters and Johnson in the 1960s – which measured men's and women's sexual responses clinically – has looked at the physical changes in an older man's sexual response. Masters' and Johnson's research is based on a small sample: only 19 men of 51-60, 14 men of 61-70 and 6 men over 71. Their observations showed that an older man takes longer to achieve an erection – minutes rather than seconds – and the erection may not be so hard as that of a young man. There is also some reduction in the volume of seminal fluid: past 50 the ejaculate measures 1-3 millilitres instead of the young man's 3-5 millilitres. Ejaculation is delayed.

Orgasm may feel different for the older man: whereas young men experience a few seconds just before ejaculation when they know orgasm is inevitable and they can't control it, older men do not notice this sensation so strongly. The forcefulness of ejaculation is also reduced, there are fewer contractions of the penile muscles and older men lose their erection more rapidly.

There is also a longer period before another erection is possible – while a young man may achieve another erection within minutes, in an older man it may be a matter of hours.

On studying the literature, it seems that there is a lot of erroneous information in circulation about sexuality and age. On the one hand, books reiterate that older people can have sex too and enjoy it; on the other they stress the fact that older people may have physical problems and that sex doesn't necessarily have to involve orgasm, penetration or even erection. One American book on 'mid life sexuality' said that men over 60 did not experience erection of the nipples or men over 50 contractions of the muscles surrounding the anus at orgasm, and that men in their fifties and sixties are unable to have erections within 12-24 hours of ejaculation. Many men in this age group with active sex lives say this is not so. 'I wonder who they were using for subjects,' said one, and another wondered about the effect of scientific testing on a man's performance and responses.

A West German book on male sexual problems confidently asserts that 'fewer than 10 per cent of men over 60 have normal sexual potency (defined as having normal sexual intercourse without difficulty at least once a month)'. One wonders what kind of a sample they were using – perhaps men who were ill in hospital, but certainly not the husbands of younger women! An expert in ageing gave the figures as 10-15 per cent of men being impotent at 45, 20 per cent at 60 and 80-85 per cent at the age of 85.

Impotence, however, has much more to do with psychology or lack of a suitable partner than with physiology. Although ageing does have some effect on erection, Masters and Johnson write that the male 'does not lose his facility for erection at any time.' Sex in the older man may become less vigorous, but it does not have to become any less pleasurable for himself or for his partner.

In a healthy man, active sex can continue into old age. There is evidence that the more sexually active a man is, the less likely he is to lose his potency. The root of most impotence, at any age, is psychological rather than physical. Masters and Johnson wrote that impotence in older men is mainly caused by 'sexual boredom and fear of failure'. In many marriages it is the woman who loses interest in sex and the man feels unable to insist. And society's attitude that sex between older people is somehow not nice doesn't help older people to maintain a satisfying sex life into old age.

A study of the frequency of sexual intercourse in later life by Pfeiffer, printed in the *American Journal of Psychology*, shows that while half the men aged 51-55 have sex once a week, this has fallen to 26 per cent by 66-71. However, this was more often than the women of the same age. While two-thirds of the men in their early sixties were still sexually active, only one-fifth of the women reported ongoing sexual activity. The authors conclude that this may largely be the result of women marrying older men who became ill or died. Or it may be that some men would not admit to lack of potency, even to a survey. (See also Chapter 7.)

Sexual problems

It is true that a lot of older men retire from sexual activity or develop sexual problems. Sometimes this is because the wife does not want sex. This may be because she has hang-ups about sex, because she does not love her partner or the relationship has deteriorated into boredom and lack of desire, or because she feels that sex is inappropriate for someone of her age. This is why so many marriages to younger women act as a tonic for older men's sex lives.

But a diminution of desire can affect men, too. Some men in a long-standing marriage feel that sex has become a burden, and engage in it only through a sense of duty or to spare their partner's feelings. At the beginning of a relationship, novelty and mutual absorption create an excitement which is often expressed in sex. But as this fades over the years, the man becomes more interested in work or hobbies and sex can become a chore.

Men also may develop sexual problems because of fears about the decline in their sexual powers with age. It is easy for a cycle of failure to be set up after just one or two episodes when a man fails to make love to his wife. Perhaps they attempt love-making when he is tired, has drunk too much, or is worried about a situation at work. He cannot get an erection, or loses it before he has completed sexual intercourse. He is nervous about this, and this sets up a pattern of stress and fear of failure that makes him fail second time round as well.

Most women can help a man out of this cycle if they accept the situation and don't put pressure on him to achieve an erection and have full sexual intercourse, The most successful technique used to cure psychological impotence is known as sensate focus. The couple do not attempt intercourse, but stroke and caress one another, first without touching the genitals, and then more intimately. With the stress of worrying about performance removed, most men find they are easily aroused. Some find that the fact that intercourse has been forbidden makes it more exciting for them, and they resume full intercourse faster than the therapist has 'allowed'. (See also Chapter 7).

Another problem for older men – and women – is that society views sex as being for young people. Sex is associated with young bodies, often idealised in the beautiful models and film-stars who parade before us in advertisements and on television. Sex for older people is hidden away.

The fact that older people have sex and enjoy it too – often as much or more than the young – is something that is not often talked about. During a television show on older parenthood, with a studio audience, a man of 50 whose wife had a young baby couldn't help blurting out as a teenager was talking: 'The trouble is you young people think you invented sex. I assure you we were doing exactly what you're doing 30 years ago, and we're still doing it now!' An older man with a young wife and baby is announcing to the world that he is still sexually active, and the world doesn't always like it very much.

Couples in marriages where there is a big age gap have to accept that they are going to receive odd looks and make the best of it. 'You just have to laugh and carry on,' says Marjorie. 'Don't give a damn about what other people think, it's their problem, not yours.'

Then there is the stereotype of the 'dirty old man.' There is felt to be something wrong, out of place, in an older man who is interested in sex, especially in sex with a younger woman. Some older men feel anxious about making a sexual approach to a younger woman for this reason, unless they are certain that she is interested in them or unless they have tremendous self-confidence. Perhaps this is one reason why so many marriages of older men and younger women take place among the rich and famous!

The sexless marriage

The opposite stereotype to that of the 'dirty old man' is that of the sexless older man and the sexless marriage. Writers like Defoe in *Moll Flanders* have written of women who earn their living from sex and find security and love in relationships with older men who do not make sexual demands upon them, thus showing them respect and love.

An American *Family Circle* survey based on interviews carried out by the Family Therapy Institute of the Western Psychology Institute, with 100 couples at different ages from their twenties to their sixties, looked at long-lasting and happy marriages and concluded that 'neither great sex nor any sex at all is crucial for a happy marriage.' Perhaps this is even more true of second and age-gap marriages. A Canadian study of 200 women found that only 33 per cent gave 'love' as the main reason for remarrying, the rest ticking liking/caring, security, social pressures, and loneliness as the main reasons, perhaps making for less sexy but more realistic marriages.

In some marriages sex becomes less important with the passing of time. Couples of the same age may both reach a stage where companionship is more important than sexual pleasure. Enid Bagnold describes this very well in her autobiography, when she writes: 'It's not until sex has died out between a man and a woman that they can really love . . . when I look back on the pain of sex, the love like a wild fox so ready to bite, the antagonism that sits like a twin beside love, and contrast it with affection, so deeply unrepeatable, of two people who have lived a life together, it's the affection I find richer (But then she's old, one must say).'

In some marriages sex is not an issue. Olivia, in her mid 30s, married a man in his 70s. 'We are good friends,' she says, "we enjoy being together, he gives me security and I am a companion for him . . . we are both happy with the relationship as it is.'

This kind of companionship is less likely to occur when there is a big age gap; problems may arise when one party is no longer interested in sex and the other is. Most couples reach an accommodation in such matters but where there is an inequality in age there are more likely to be hidden fears. The woman may be insecure and concerned about the possibility of her husband's sexual powers fading and this may lead to lack of open communication and thus to other problems in the relationship.

Health and sex life

While there should be no problem with sex *per se* if a man is healthy, the risks of illness clearly increase with age, and this can affect a man's sex life. Coronary heart disease is one of the most common causes of death and ill health in Western men. In the 45-64 age range, men are at three times as great a risk of heart disease as women. A heart attack can be a devastating event for any man and often affects his sexuality for a number of reasons, most psychological. Recent studies show that 60-75 per cent of couples decrease or stop sexual activity altogether after the man has suffered a heart attack. (See also chapter 7.)

Most of the reasons for stopping sex are to do with fear — fear that exertion during sex will lead to another heart attack. After a wait of 16 weeks or so, most men are told they can resume sexual intercourse. During averagely active sex the heart beat ranges from 90 to 160 beats a minute — the same as light to moderate activity, and should therefore present no problems. Couples are often told to use sexual positions in which the man does not exert himself so much and lies down comfortably without contorting his body in any way.

Most doctors, however, fail to realise the full effect of fear on the sex lives of couples when the man has had a heart attack. Often, inadequate counselling is given. As one woman, aged 40, whose husband had a heart attack at 52, recalls: 'Nobody really helped us think it through. We were both terrified. The doctor told us to avoid the man on top position and though we didn't always make love this way it was our preferred position. Me on top seemed to make him feel even less adequate. Fear obviously doesn't help one to feel sexy. Both of us had problems. I think also at the back of one's mind there is a link between sex and death – it's hard to deal with this rationally. It was only after we had succeeded a few times and nothing terrible happened that we began to feel a bit better about it and began to relax and enjoy things again.'

Sometimes, remarks by a doctor can make things worse. One doctor told his patient recovering from a heart attack that it was very unlikely that he would have a heart attack during sexual intercourse, but that if he did, he could comfort himself that it was a great way to go! This thoughtless remark came back to him time and time again when he wanted to make love to his wife and created problems for them both.

Fertility not virility

Fertility is another question that may concern a woman married to an older man. As men age the sperm count does gradually decrease, and male fertility usually ends in the mid seventies, though men in their nineties have been known to father children. Charlie Chaplin and Pierre Trudeau both fathered children in their seventies. Decreases in the male hormone testosterone take place very gradually with age and there are wide variations from man to man. Certainly most men in their fifties will be able to father a child without problems; most men in their sixties and many in their seventies are capable of becoming fathers. Examples of men who fathered children later in life are the artist Picasso and cellist Pablo Casals.

Unlike women, for whom the risk of giving birth to a handicapped child increases markedly in their late thirties and forties, older men seem not to run the risk of having a handicapped child. However, there is some evidence that there are a few conditions which are linked to an older father. One is a rare form of dwarfism called achondroplasia. There is also some evidence that Down's Syndrome is slightly more common in children conceived when the man is over 55.

Physically based impotence

There are some illnesses which lead to physically based impotence. Diabetes is one, although usually the disease has to be quite severe or long-lasting before problems occur. Other causes of physical impotence are some circulatory problems, radical surgery, trauma or pelvic injuries, hormonal problems, and multiple sclerosis. Alcoholism can also result in impaired sexual performance and impotence.

In many cases it is the drugs used to treat these conditions that can cause problems; it is always worth discussing this with your doctor, to make sure that, where possible, drugs are chosen which do not affect sexuality and are given at as low a dose as possible. Drugs which affect potency in men include diuretics (often used in the treatment of heart disease), some drugs used in the treatment of high blood pressure, opiates (used for pain relief), sex hormones used to treat hormonal disorders, a common drug used in the treatment of Parkinson's disease, and some drugs used to treat mental illness.

Men who suffer from impotence for physical reasons may still be able to enjoy sex. Just because a couple cannot have full sexual intercourse, they can still cuddle, caress one another, and find other ways of stimulating one another, such as mutual masturbation, oral sex, using sex toys and erotic literature. A man can still feel very pleasurable sensations without getting a firm erection and he can still give pleasure to and satisfy his partner. It is also possible for many men to have an orgasm without having an erection.

For those who feel that vaginal penetration is vital to their sexual fulfilment, physically based impotence can be treated with penile implants and with drugs. An increasingly widely used treatment is the injection of papaverine (a derivative of opium) into the spongy part of the penis, which causes a long-lasting erection. Once the correct dose for the individual has been established, men can be taught to give themselves the injection before they want to make love. Apparently this is not painful, once the man has learned how to do it correctly.

47

Prostate problems

One of the commonest complaints for middle-aged and older men – and which causes a great deal of anxiety about sexuality and fertility – is enlargement of the prostate gland. In all men over the age of 45 the prostate does enlarge to a greater or less extent, but in some men the gland enlarges in such a way that it presses on the urethra, the tube which carries urine from the bladder through the penis, restricting the flow of urine. If untreated, this obstruction can cause bladder infections and stones and, sometimes, eventually kidney damage. Early symptoms are those of bladder stress – the need to get up, sometimes several times, to pass water at night, frequent urination during the day, impaired stream, small volume of urine passed, occasionally the need to urinate suddenly or urgently.

Until quite recently, the only available treatment has been surgery – one reason why men tend to put up with their symptoms rather than seeking medical help. But now, although surgery will remain the treatment for most men for some years to come, drug treatments are being developed and outpatient hyperthermia (heat treatment) is gradually becoming available in some areas.

There are a lot of misconceptions about prostate problems, and one that should be corrected straightaway is that the prostate operation is likely to cause impotence or other sexual problems. However, one likely side-effect of the operation is functional *infertility*, and any woman who wishes to have (further) children should be aware of this if her husband develops prostate problems.

The modern prostate operation, known as transurethral resection of the prostate, or TURP, involves a four- or five-day stay in hospital. During the operation an electric arc cutting device with fibre optic vision is introduced through the penis and the obstructing part of the prostate (not the entire gland) is cut away. It is a straightforward and safe operation which is usually successful in removing the obstruction and resolving the bladder problems. Most men are told to have a month off work and not to take part in strenuous activity – including sexual intercourse – for this period of time.

Infertility is a common result of the operation because semen is ejaculated back into the bladder at orgasm instead of outwards in the usual way. But orgasm itself is not affected, and the man's enjoyment of sex is almost always unimpaired.

If a prostate operation threatens and fertility is an issue, you should go with your husband to see the consultant to discuss the possibility of alternative treatments. Alternatively, sperm can be banked before treatment – this service is unfortunately not usually available on the NHS – or there are medical techniques which can retrieve the sperm for artificial insemination, so having another child is not absolutely ruled out.

Prostate problems however can cause difficulties in a relationship. One younger wife recalls:

'At first he concealed it from me. I think because it was an 'old man's disease,' although he was only in his early fifties. The problem was, I wanted another child. When we were told he should have the operation they didn't even bother to tell us that he might become infertile. When he asked about sex, the doctor just said, 'Oh, it won't affect your sexuality.' I only found out about the fertility problem through reading up in a book in the library.

'The problem is, I think the doctors think of it as an old man's operation too. The doctor was very taken aback when we said we wanted more children; he didn't know what to suggest. There were some amusing incidents later on, which we can laugh about now. After the operation they said he shouldn't have sex till he felt 'up to it.' The doctor thought this would be about a month; in fact it was about 10 days after the operation. It was really hard for us to resist the temptation. Nobody gave us any real advice because I don't think they knew the answers and they thought anyone who had the operation would be old and not very interested in sex.'

Secondary infertility and its treatment

Infertility in men is usually not age-related, but it can be a problem just as it is with younger men. A man whose sperm count was low but adequate when he was in his twenties may find that by his late forties or fifties his fertility has dropped too low to make pregnancy likely.

Older men may suffer from what is known as secondary infertility when they have succeeded in fathering a child before. Secondary infertility can be caused by a falling sperm count, by previous sexually transmitted infections such as gonorrhoea, or a varicocele, a kind of varicose vein in the testicle.

The problem with male infertility is that it is poorly understood and little can be done to correct it in most cases. Hormonal treatments aimed at increasing the sperm count have had limited success and it has even been argued that the chances of conceiving are lowered by some drug treatments. Surgery to correct a varicocele does have some degree of success, and surgery can repair tubes blocked by infections in some cases.

One technique which has been used with some success to help infertility when the man has a low sperm count is the 'split ejaculate' technique. The first part of the man's semen which is ejaculated is richest in sperm. If the first part of several ejaculates is pooled together, then stored, and then introduced into the woman's vagina through artificial insemination, the chances of pregnancy may be increased.

The 'test-tube baby' technique or IVF (in vitro fertilisation), and a variation of this procedure known as GIFT (gamete intra-fallopian transfer), both offer a greater chance of fertilisation for a man with a low sperm count because the sperm can be mixed with the egg rather than making the long and difficult journey through the woman's reproductive system.

Another cause of infertility in older men is vasectomy. A man who remarried may have had a vasectomy in his first marriage at a time when he thought he would want no more children; this then raises problems in a second marriage.

Vasectomies can be reversed, and there has been a growing demand for vasectomy reversal operations. The Marie Stopes Clinic in London now does an average of half a dozen every week. The problem is that even when the vasectomy has been successfully reversed surgically, in up to half of cases fertility does not return. This is because when a man has a vasectomy, sperm have to be reabsorbed by the body instead of ejaculated, and the body can produce antibodies to the sperm which continue to be produced even after the vasectomy has been surgically reversed.

A study of men seeking donor insemination after failed vasectomy reversal at St George's Hospital, London showed that most of the men were considerably older than their wives, with an average age of 43 as compared with the wives' average age of 29 – a gap of 14 years. The age gap found between other couples seeking donor insemination for reasons other than vasectomy was only two years.

Infertility is very distressing for a man whatever his age, because society tends to equate virility with fertility, and men have a hard time admitting that they may have a problem. The older man may be even more sensitive about this than younger men, partly because he comes from a generation when sex was not discussed as freely as it is now, and partly because he may have fears anyway about his virility or about how other people see him.

While in most infertile marriages, people tend to assume it's the wife's problem, people may not think the same if the man is in his fifties or sixties.

Artificial insemination

If a young wife is desperate to have a child, artificial insemination by donor, usually known today as DI (donor insemination) means that a woman can conceive and bear a child although it is not her partner's biological child. DI is not actually a cure for infertility, it simply bypasses it. Most children are not told that their biological father is an unknown donor and there is a lot of secrecy surrounding it, which can create problems as the child grows up.

Helen opted for AID because her husband had had a vasectomy after his two children were born to his first wife. An attempt to reverse it failed and Andrew, aged 51, agreed that Helen at 33 should have the opportunity to become a mother before it was too late.

Helen says, 'Everything has been fine. Andrew accepted Samuel from the start. After all, he accepts that I have to get on with his step-daughters and that we're not a conventional family. He says that anyway Sam feels just like his son, he's not aware of any difference, and that he'd love Sam anyway because he's mine. I don't know if I will ever tell Sam. By the time he's grown up Andrew will be 70 or may even not be here any more and there wouldn't seem to be much point in upsetting things. As far as I'm concerned Andrew is his dad and that's all there is to it.'

An optimistic note

Any fears an older man may have about infertility are usually not founded; nor are fears about his virility. One thing that seems certain is that the more a man has satisfying sexual relations, the more virile he will remain; as the old adage goes, 'If you don't use it, you lose it.' The *Handbook of the Psychology of Aging** puts it more scientifically: 'Perhaps the most significant finding in the current literature is that amounts of past sexual activity and enjoyment are excellent predictors of sexual activity and enjoyment in old age.'

Many men who marry younger wives say that their sex lives are much better, and that they are having sex as frequently, or more so, as they did when younger.

'Quite honestly it's a real turn-on for me having a younger woman in bed with me,' says one older husband, in his late fifties, 'How could anyone not find her attractive, desire her,

---

* *Handbook of the Psychology of Aging*, Ed. James E Birren and K Warner Schaie. Van Nostrand Reinhold Co, 1977.

want to make love to her? We've been married for 10 years and we still behave like a honeymoon couple. I have never found sex so satisfying before.'

Chapter 5

PEER, PARENT OR FRIEND?

'You can't be a peer. You can't be a parent. It took me five years to figure it out.'

CHERIE BURNS
Stepmotherhood

Statistics show that of men in their forties who marry women 10 or 20 years younger, about three-quarters will have been married before. This means that most women who marry older men will inherit an ex-wife and also children from their partner's former marriage.

For the second wife there are two main problems to be faced – the ex-wife, and any stepchildren. A third problem facing women who marry a divorced older man, is that many people will assume that the younger woman was responsible for tempting the man away from his former wife – a belief which may persist whatever is said and whatever is the truth. This can make relationships with in-laws, other relatives and friends of the family very tricky.

Usually the ex-wife is older and more mature that the new wife and thus represents a threat. No matter how little a second wife sees her – or even if she doesn't see her at all – she will be talked about and has a physical embodiment in the children of the marriage. She is usually a force to be reckoned with.

Some women find they resent the time the previous wife had with their husband, and, as one second wife put it, 'I resent the fact that she had his youth.'

The first wife will have had experiences with her husband which can never be repeated, such as the birth of his first child. Even if the second marriage is clearly happier than the first, the former wife often seems to have more status simply from having been the first. For this reason many second wives find it hard to shake off the shadow of their predecessor.

Christobel, who married a man 15 years older, remembers going through a phase when she was desperate to see her husband's ex. 'We had never met. I suppose because, since there were no children, there was never any reason to, but I just wanted to see her, to satisfy my curiosity. Once I went and sat in the car outside her house all evening waiting for her to come out, but she never did. On another occasion I went and hid behind a hedge, hoping to catch a glimpse of her, until someone came and asked me what I was doing. To this day I have never seen her.'

Marjorie, too, recalls being obsessed for a time with her husband's ex. 'I used to go through all the photograph albums looking at their wedding photos, photos of their honeymoon, of his wife with their first baby, happy holiday snaps. He told me that he didn't love her any more, had no more interest in her, and I believed him, but *I* was still fascinated by her. I can't really explain what was behind it. Perhaps it was just insecurity that if he had once loved his wife and could leave her then he could do the same to me. So I looked for evidence in these photos that he didn't love her as he now loved me.'

Frozen in time – and memory

If the previous wife is dead, this can lead to other difficulties. Heather, 40, says: 'People I know who have married divorced men have said to me, "well, at least you don't have to worry about his ex-wife because she's dead." But really it's much worse. They can usually compare themselves favourably with the ageing older ex, but all I have are these photos of Jane frozen in a book, always looking beautiful and young. He will never say anything against her, no "I love you more than I loved her." Her family all expect me to keep the house as it was – I get remarks like, "Why have you moved Jane's piano?" She has become idolised by everyone and I feel, because I'm alive and human and make mistakes, I can't keep up with this paragon of virtue.'

In Daphne du Maurier's novel, *Rebecca*, this malign influence of a dead former wife is vividly portrayed. The second Mrs de Winter, aged 21 as compared with her husband Maxim's 41, moves into the splendid house called Manderley and is vividly aware of her predecessor's presence. She believes her husband is still in love with her memory. 'Whenever you spoke to me or looked at me, walked with me in the garden, sat down to dinner, I felt you were saying to yourself, "This I did with Rebecca, and this, and this."' The novel ends with the wish of a woman in this situation fulfilled when the husband, Maxim, declares, 'You thought I loved Rebecca? . . . I hated her . . . We never loved each other, never had one moment of happiness together.'

In real life, however, nobody is usually perfectly loved or hated; people feel a mixture of the two emotions. Carol, married to a divorced man 12 years older than herself, says, 'I don't mind that he still has some affectionate feelings towards his ex-wife. After all, he shared his life with her for 15 years so he's bound to feel something. I would feel more worried about him as a person if he didn't feel anything at all about her.'

Strong feelings of hate felt by a man towards his ex-wife usually mean that something hasn't been resolved between the two, and often causes problems in a second marriage. 'He spends a lot of time thinking about ways he can get back at or humiliate his ex, who left him after a long affair with a married man,' says Vivienne. 'I say, put that all in the past, you've got me now, but I know he still broods. Since there is a daughter, he has to have some contact with his ex-wife, and I find this very difficult. I think the resentment he feels is bad for his daughter, too.'

There is little a second wife can do in these circumstances, except to talk about it, or suggest that her husband has counselling if there is a major unresolved problem.

The wicked stepmother

Stepmotherhood is never easy, whatever the circumstances, whatever the age of stepmother and children. The very word stepmother has a bad feel to it, mainly because of all the fairy stories of wicked stepmothers. Psychoanalysts say that the stepmother myth is actually a way the child has of dealing with the good and bad aspects of the mother, but in days when maternal mortality and death from other causes was high there were probably a lot of stepmothers, and they were probably no better at this difficult and demanding role than are today's stepmothers. At least the old-fashioned stepmother knew what she was doing – taking over the dead mother's role with the children – a situation which is now quite rare. Today, most stepmothers have to share that role with the real mother. They are not so sure where they stand.

Some stepmothers try to deal with the problem by keeping the stepchildren more or less out of their lives, especially if the children are practically grown up. This doesn't work; even if you don't see them often, they have a way of intruding into the marriage. Others make the mistake of thinking that they must love their stepchildren and their stepchildren love them; this may happen, but usually it is unrealistic. Mandy, 30, whose husband Bob is 42 and has two boys, has been married five years. She says, 'When I married him I thought I was going to love them, I really did. I tried so hard, and what I got was rejection all the way. They didn't really need me, they resented me, I made a fool of myself. Then I went through a phase of really hating them because they had rejected me. Now, five years later, we just get on. We respect one another, and really, I think that's the best we could expect – in fact, it's a good thing. We respect one another as stepmother and children, and I don't pretend to be anything else to them.'

And what do the children themselves say? Mostly, children accept and get on with what happens because they have no other choice. There are probably very few children whose parents' marriage had broken up who wouldn't prefer them to be together again. Children can be very cruel and critical of their parents, and step-parents too. As one stepdaughter said, 'The advice I'd give is; don't expect to like one another. Don't even try. Just get on with it and then if you don't pretend things you might find you rub along all right.'

Ruth, a teenage stepdaughter wrote, 'Fortunately my step-mother has never behaved maternally towards me, possibly because we are so close in age. She is only six years older than me, young enough to be my sister. My stepmother has just given birth to their second child. My father, now in his sixties, appears to be producing his own grandchildren.'

Adult or teenage stepchildren

Pamela is 47 and her husband 68. She writes, 'My role as "stepmother" to six "children" aged 26 to 39 is very strange. There was strain between Peter and all the children before I came on the scene, so my relationship with them is coloured by this. I tend to feel angry with them for not having stood by their father when he was going through a very bad time. I think the best I can say about this is that all relationships in their family were distorted and upset by the atrocious deterioration of the parents' marriage.'

Coping with an ex-wife and a stepfamily is never easy, but for women who marry older men, it may be even more difficult. The former marriage is often longer lived, and it is harder to cope with an ex-wife of 20 years standing than one who was only married to one's partner for a short time. Also the children are often older, and many wives of older men are closer in age to their partner's children than they are to him. This can make it doubly difficult to form a suitable relationship with the children. As one woman in this situation said, 'I was only 24. David and his wife were 20 years older than I was and yet with all their maturity and experience, and having brought up their children over 15 years, even they could hardly handle them. How was I supposed to cope?'

Sarah's story highlights many of the dilemmas of this situation very well: 'When I married Martin I knew he had a difficult relationship with his ex-wife and that he had two teenage daughters. I didn't actually meet them till after we had fixed a wedding date; perhaps this was a mistake.

'Martin was 49 and I was 32. He had been married to Cathy for nearly 20 years. He left her just before he met me but Cathy assumed that he must have left her for me. I suppose she was going through the menopause and her daughters were going off to university and becoming independent just when all this happened. She really hated me. She probably prejudiced her daughters against me from the outset. There are 14 years between Liz, the youngest daughter, and me and 17 between me and Martin. Obviously I cannot have any kind of parental relationship with my stepdaughters; I am far too young to have been their mother.'

If the children from the first marriage are still dependent, the new wives often find themselves having to take responsibility for the children at least at weekends or other times when the children visit their father. For a woman who hasn't had a family of her own, this can be very difficult.

Pauline, 24, married Martin, 41, whose two children were 11 and 13. 'I found it impossible at first,' recalls Pauline. 'The children were both at very difficult ages. They resented me, and everything I did was no good. I didn't make the mistake of telling them what to do – I tried to be friendly – but Martin didn't help very much. He would just get on with all the things he normally did and leave all the responsibility to me, which, since I'd never had to deal with children before, I found very difficult.'

Coping with resentment

Many second wives find that having the stepchildren with them is not too much of a problem, or that they are prepared to put enough into the relationship to make it work. Others, especially when they feel they are on to a losing wicket, decide to step back. 'After a while I decided that it wasn't working and that I didn't see why I should lay myself open to being abused and trampled on by them,' says Claire. 'I used to make my own arrangements for when they were coming and leave them to my husband. It worked out much better that way; after all, it was him they were coming to see, not me.'

Some stepmothers find that they resent the time that their partner spends with the stepchildren. Sue used to find herself waiting angrily for his return when he had gone to visit them in the former matrimonial home, wondering what they had all been doing. 'Once I realised this was a difficult situation for me, I always arranged to go out and do something for myself when he was visiting them,' she recalls. 'That way I wasn't so resentful of the time he was away from me.'

If the children are young, the second wife does have the advantage – or disadvantage – of having to make some kind of relationship with them by spending time with them and caring for them. When the children are grown up, a great gulf can result. 'They simply won't have anything to do with me,' says Anne, who at 35 is married to a man of 50. 'They lead their own lives and have very much sided with their mother. They see their father only at family occasions – to which I'm not invited – and they arrange to meet him sometimes for lunch or in the evening. Obviously this leads to a lot of resentment on my part, though I can hardly ask Mike to break off all contact with them if they refuse to meet me; that would probably be what would happen.'

Not all second wives resent the time their partners spend with their stepchildren. Others are sad that, because of divorce, their partners become virtual strangers to their children. Perhaps there is some guilt at work here.

Losing touch

One stepmother writes of the sadness she feels that her husband doesn't have a closer relationship with the children of his first marriage. 'His daughter wrote to him once, saying, "I feel as if you divorced me as well when you divorced Mum." I think in some ways she was right; when we married and had children together all his energies went into us and he didn't have much time to see his older children, who he considered were grown up and maybe didn't need him so much. The sad thing is they hurt one another; he complains they never ring him up, they obviously feel he doesn't make the effort to contact them. I encourage him to, I often nag him to ring them up, but I'm sure they actually think that it's me who's preventing them from seeing him.'

His and hers

Many second wives do feel guilty at the break-up of the first marriage and feel they have to compensate to the stepchildren for the loss of their previous home. Because of this, some second wives put up with difficult behaviour and awkward situations which they would not tolerate in their own children. Family relationships can be even more strained when there are children from both sides of the marriage. (See Chapter 6.)

Gail was a 55-year-old widow when she married a widower of 68. She inherited three grown up stepchildren, some of whom had children of their own. 'My eldest step-grand-daughter is two years older than my daughter,' she says. 'I don't think they can get used to me. At first they were relieved, I think, that Gordon had found somebody to look after him. But then they realised he wasn't around so much for them and they resented that. We get along all right but they are always ringing up and wanting something. Actually I'm wondering if we wouldn't be better off if we moved away and were a bit more distant.'

Stepmothers are often resentful of the fact that they actually have no legal or other rights or responsibilities over their stepchildren. This may be true even if the father has custody or care and control of the children and they live with him and the stepmother. Decisions about education, medical treatment and other important areas will rest with the child's natural parents, regardless of who the children live with. Access arrangements, too, are fixed between the parents.

'What drove me mad was that nobody ever consulted me about the visiting arrangements, even though I had to be involved,' says Susie. 'Since my husband doesn't drive I had to do all the to-ing and fro-ing, otherwise he wouldn't have got to see the children. He had them every other weekend and saw them once a week and this was all arranged in advance. It meant we had a completely inflexible life and this didn't suit me at all, especially since I work freelance and never know when I'm going to be working in advance. Needless to say, his ex-wife wasn't prepared to do anything that might suit me.'

If there is such unwillingness to compromise, there is little the second wife can do but learn to live with the situation and try not to resent it.

When a child is ill there can be problems, too. 'I looked after her, I became very fond of her, and then when she was in hospital I was completely cut out,' recalls Rosie, whose stepdaughter was in hospital for a month following a serious accident. 'Thank God she was with her father and not with me when the accident happened. Nobody thought to consult me or inform me about what was happening and of course I didn't have the right to participate in any decisions about her treatment. I found this very hard and very painful; it reinforced the fact that she was part of my husband and his ex and not part of me.'

Money matters

Finances also have a bearing on the happiness of second marriages. There has been some criticism of the changes in the divorce law which mean that a former wife no longer has a 'meal ticket for life'. Where marriages have been short and there are no children, divorce courts are not generous to the wife; this enables wealthy older men to marry and divorce a series of young wives without serious financial pressures. Since the 1984 Matrimonial and Family Proceedings Act, they have not been obliged to maintain the wife in the same financial position to which she had become accustomed during the marriage.

However, where there are children, or where the marriage has been long-standing and the wife hasn't worked, the husband often loses out. The matrimonial home has to stay with the wife and children until the latter have completed full-time education. If the wife agrees to sell and move to a smaller or cheaper home, the bulk of the money resulting from the sale of the property will go to her and the children. The husband will have to pay maintenance for the children, and, if the wife is not working or works very little, alimony too.

Angie, 35, and her husband Graham, 52, lived in a one-bedroomed flat for several years while waiting for his divorce to come through. He had three teenage children, still at school, and his wife opposed the divorce for the full five years. Of course we were happy together, but it was very difficult for us,' says Angie. 'We never had any money and I worked desperately hard, knowing that I was subsidising Graham's ex-wife by doing so, because all his money went on them. It made it difficult for him to see the children because they couldn't all three come to the flat very easily; there simply wasn't room to fit five people round the table. We never had holidays and we couldn't afford to do a lot of the things that young married couples would do.'

The constant drain on finances can cause resentment as time goes on. 'I remember when my husband got divorced, his lawyer warned him about being too generous with his ex-wife, because it could have repercussions for his second marriage,' recalls Marjorie. 'At the time he just thought, what the hell, it doesn't matter. Let her have the house and car, and everything, it's happiness that counts. But it was difficult because we couldn't afford to buy a decent place to live and then I had to go back to work after I had my first baby – something I didn't really want to do and which his wife hadn't had to do – because we never had any money. I think in the end he realised that his generosity had indeed been a mistake.'

Money is often one of the main causes of resentment between first and second families. If the husband has children from his first marriage, there can be unpleasant scenes in which the children are asked by the ex-wife to try to find out how much money the second wife is earning, if they are planning a holiday, if they've spent money on the house and so on.

Children whose parents divorce sometimes feel short-changed of love and money forms a convenient substitute, so they can become very mercenary. Marjorie recalls, 'My teenage stepson used to get pocket money from us and pocket money from his mother, too. When we took him on holiday he concealed from us that his mother had given him money to buy presents and send postcards with, so he got money out of us, too. At birthdays and Christmas he used to tell us how much his mother was spending and usually exaggerated. It was very difficult because if we tried to discuss it with his mother it resulted in long conversations about money, the very thing we actually wanted to avoid.'

Coping with jealousy

It's not just money that makes for difficulties – no matter how much everyone might want to pretend otherwise, there is obvious jealousy at work when a man has a second wife. If he has a daughter, and a daughter close in age, how will she react to this new woman in her father's arms? It isn't easy for either woman. What is one to make of the feelings of the second wife, who, opening the door at the wedding party to an old friend of her husband's hears her ask, 'And how is Susie reacting to her father's wedding?' And what is one to make of the feelings of the 15 year old who has been used to sitting on her father's lap, seeing his new wife, barely five years older, doing the same?

Obviously, dealing with such situations is difficult. Kathy says, 'I know that my stepdaughter was the most important person in my husband's life till I came along. Now I am the most important person; that's the way it has to be. His stepdaughter is growing up now and will eventually go off and make her own relationships. But I know it must be hard for her.'

If the step-children are still young enough for there to be a big age gap, then there is some hope of a stepmother forming an adult-child, if not mother-child, bond with their stepchild. This is particularly true when the stepmother has to do a lot of the caring for them, even if this is only part-time, for instance at weekends. Where the age-gap is much smaller, the best a stepmother can hope to achieve is a kind of tolerance and friendship. But even this has its pitfalls. 'My husband used to hate it when we got together and chatted about pop music, clothes and the like,' says Louise. 'I think he couldn't bear to be reminded that his daughter and I were actually the same generation.'

Sometimes the relationship starts off well but runs into problems later. This is sometimes because young children have little interest in family possessions, but when they are older realise that money and family heirlooms are likely to pass to the second wife and her family rather than to themselves. Barbara was 39 and her husband 62 when they married; he had a 30-year-old daughter from his previous marriage. 'She seemed to be delighted he had met me, it was less of a responsibility for her. As we were so close in age I hoped I had acquired a friend and initially her invitations to come and stay in London and so on bore this out. However, in time this totally changed, and I was seen as 'the grasping wife' and cold-shouldered by her.'

Others find the relationship works more smoothly; 'None of our children have ever questioned us about the financial arrangements we made for them after our demise or shown any resentment, and they are genuinely pleased that we have found personal happiness.'

Summing up

So what can second wives do to make life easier for themselves? First and most important – talk about things. If you get your feelings out into the open they are less likely to fester and cause problems in your own marriage. Second marriages are statistically more likely to fail than first ones, so you need to keep one step ahead. Feeling secure in your new relationship is the most important thing, and being able to put the past behind you. You should consciously avoid fuelling the fire. It is all too easy to use an ex-wife as a scapegoat for everything that goes wrong in this second marriage, so try to avoid this. Concentrate on the present and future together – the past is over, unless you insist on hurling it into the present for fresh examination.

Chapter 6

A CHILD
OF YOUR OWN?

'You don't object to an aged parent, I hope?'

WEMMICK IN CHARLES DICKENS
Great Expectations

One of the major hurdles to be faced when a younger woman marries an older man is the question of whether to have children together. This can often be a problem, because for most younger women the answer will be a definite 'yes', but for many older men, the marriage is their second and they will have had children before. Other older men who have been bachelors for many years may find the idea of having a family quite threatening.

If this hasn't been discussed before the couple married, problems can result. 'I never really discussed the question of children with Jeff,' says Wendy, 35. 'He'd had two children who were now teenagers and I suppose I thought we would have at least one child together. But when I suggested having a baby he got really alarmed. He said, "Oh no, not broken nights and nappies and sick all over my clothes all over again." First-time-round fathers are probably a bit starry-eyed about becoming a father. Second time round they know what it's all about and it's harder to let yourself in for it.'

Beliza Ann Furman, founder of the American-based Wives Of Older Men, says a husband's concern about a second family can be a major stumbling block. 'The fact that your husband grew up on Sinatra and you grew up on Elton John is easier to resolve than whether or not to have a baby,' she says. 'When you're in your early twenties you may think you don't want to have kids, but in all likelihood, as your biological clock ticks away, you'll change your mind.' Often this is about the time the older husband might be thinking of retiring. 'The last thing he'd want to worry about at that point in his life is how to pay for the education of an offspring.'

Finances may play a very important part, as we saw in Chapter 5, as well as worries about the effects on the existing children of one or both partners and whether there will be jealousy and resentment. Jealousy there may be – but there may be love too.

Doreen had a negative experience. 'I think my husband's first two sons felt they had missed out on him,' she says. 'He was busy with his career when they were small and then in their teens he was too busy with us to do a lot with them, though he did sometimes take them to football matches and he did once take them on a week's cycling holiday. But they see him being so close to our son Daniel and I think they do resent it a lot. They always notice if we've bought him anything expensive and comment on it, and we have to be very careful not to spend more money on Daniel at Christmas.'

Susie had the opposite experience. 'I always found things were a bit difficult with my stepson and stepdaughter until we had our own child. They were 16 and 11 at the time. I remember they came to see him in the hospital and they were both delighted and fascinated and intrigued that he looked so like his dad – and indeed, like they did when they were babies. I remember I at once felt closer to them – I thought, well, we are all related now, there is a blood link. Now Emma comes and babysits sometimes and it all works out really well.'

Marjorie found that she could use her own child as a means of expressing affection to her rather distant teenage stepson. 'The awful thing was that I could never touch or cuddle James, much as I often wanted to,' she says. 'He was too old at 12 when I first met him for me to cuddle and so it just never happened. But when I had my own child I was able to say to him, 'Go and give Jamie a kiss,' and he would do it for me.'

To have or have not

Some couples do decide not to have children. 'I imagine marrying an older man could cause problems if the woman craves for a family and the husband cannot cope with all the upheaval that would involve, especially if he has already brought up one family,' writes Ingrid. She had married older men twice, the first 26 years older, the second 14 (she had a brief marriage to a man the same age as herself when her first husband died but that was a 'disaster' which ended after five years). 'Fortunately, I never really wanted children so the problem didn't arise.'

Sarah, whose husband had three children from his first marriage, said he was adamant that he didn't want to go through all that again, but this is a decision she now regrets. 'I think we should have talked it over more and that I should have put my case more strongly,' she says. 'When I married him he made it plain that having children wasn't on the cards. I didn't mind at the time, but I do regret it now. He is likely to die well before me and I suppose I can look forward to a lonely old age.'

Janet, now 40, married her husband when she was 35 and he was 48; he had three children from his first marriage. 'It took his wife so long to agree to the divorce and we had so little money that I didn't really consider having children till it was almost too late. We did talk about it, but we were enjoying our time together and I could see that having a child would change everything. We didn't really make a concrete decision. Time just drifted by and now I think we're both too old, it would be unfair on the child. By the time the child was grown up I would be 60 and Geoff would be 73.'

Other women find that they have fewer children with an older husband than they would have done if they had a younger partner. 'We have two, and I have to say, the main reason why I don't have another is Gavin's age,' says Christobel. 'I'm only 31, and I could easily have another, but Gavin is 46 and I think he's had enough. It's all right to become a father at 40 or 45 but not at 50. It isn't fair on the child.'

There is probably little basis in this last comment, since it is in the nature of children to accept their parents as they are – young, old, rich, poor, kind, cruel, warm, cold. The emotional characteristics of a parent are far more crucial to a child's development than any possible perception that his parents are 'old'. And a healthy man of 50 probably has a life expectancy of 30 years. He is also less likely than a younger man to leave his younger wife after say 10 years' marriage, so the child is less likely to suffer the trauma of divorce.

Certainly, the majority of younger women, even if they already have had a child or children, will want to have children with their older man, and the man would be wise not to try to ignore or belittle this wish. If he wants to have children as well this can prove to be one of the main joys of such a relationship. If he doesn't, he should seriously question whether he should encourage the relationship, because unless the woman is quite sure that she does not want children by him it could become a source of much conflict and unhappiness. Women who in their mid-twenties may be convinced that they don't 'really' want children may well change their mind 10 years later.

It's best to discuss important issues like whether or not you want to have children right at the beginning before you commit yourselves. It is not something you can compromise about. Many marriages have come unstuck because the couple have avoided getting such basic disagreements out in the open for fear of jeopardising the relationship, not realising it is likely to cause more havoc later on.

Occasionally the situation is the other way round, with the husband wanting children more than his younger wife does. This was Pat's problem. She married a man 19 years older, when she was in her 20s, and although her husband had three children from his first marriage, he was keen that they should have just one together. Pat saw herself as a career woman and was ambivalent about having children. 'To be honest, I'm not sure that thinking he wouldn't mind not having children wasn't one of the factors I unconsciously weighed up in wanting to marry him.'

Pat thinks part of the problem was the 'generation gap'. 'He was happy with me, but I wanted more independence than the traditional kind of wife he had been used to, and this was part of the rift between us.' As often happens, a difference of opinion over something as fundamental as the desire to have a child or not to have a child tore apart the marriage.

A second lease of life

One of the advantages men have over women is their continuing ability to father children into middle age – indeed into old age. A recent record may have been set by Les Colley, pictured in the magazine *Marie-Claire*, in 1992, holding his eight-week-old son Oswald. Les Colley is 92, and his wife Patti is 38. Les's other son, Norman, from his first marriage, is 72.

He says, 'I could live for another 20 years, and I'm sure I will. The doctor says that I'm in better shape than a man of 60. I'm a teenager at heart.' Patti says, 'I wasn't surprised that Les could father a child. He's quite a good lover, actually, better than some younger men I've had. I think Les will live for about another 10-15 years, but it would be a pity for the baby not to see his father as he grows up.'

While some older men who have brought up one family would hate to go through the experience again at an age when most men are preparing to face grandfatherhood – an attitude that may be shared by women who have had their fill of child rearing – others are delighted at the prospect of having young children around them, even in their fifties and sixties.

'It's like being given a second lease of life,' says James, who remarried at the age of 45, when the children from his first marriage were at secondary school, and 10 years later has three little ones. 'I feel I have enjoyed this brood better, perhaps because I am less hung up about career achievement than I was 25 years ago. It also has to do with the quality of the relationship with their mother and being more in harmony with myself – I was so uncertain and restless as a younger man.'

Another man puts it even more strongly when he says, 'I feel I have been given a whole second life. I look around at my friends; their children are grown up and all they have to talk about is where they're going on holiday and where they're going to move to when they retire. Instead, I am still in the thick of things. I won't be able to retire early as some of them can. We're thinking about the new baby, about schools, about the children's future. I have more in common with the younger fathers I meet through my wife and kids that I have with a lot of my old friends.'

Chris was in his fifties when his two children were born; his wife is 24 years younger. 'I think, unquestionably, I have had more time for and enjoyed my children much more than most of the younger fathers I know. They say to me, 'Where have they gone? They've left home now and I've missed them growing up – I don't know what happened.' He says he was never aware of any problems or of a generation gap: 'I think you're just their father. Perhaps they respect you more if you're older; I don't know. We have a very good relationship. They're grown up now, I'm still working. I don't think it's much different to any other relationship between a father and his children.'

Research has shown that, on the whole, children do not improve marital happiness. The classic study of the impact of children on marriage, first done in Britain but confirmed in America, showed that married couples are happiest before the arrival of their first child. This decreases as more children are born and grow older, reaching a nadir in the children's teens, only to rise again when they all leave home.

However, this is not true of second marriages. Here, having children actually seems to increase happiness in most cases. The children of second marriages often seem much more wanted than those of the first and the parents tend to be older and more mature. These children can be a real blessing to the marriage and be a source of much happiness and pleasure.

A different kind of father

There are other concerns, however. Some wives fear that their older husbands will 'stand out' as older fathers, looking out of place at school functions and thought of as elderly by their children. In most cases, these fears prove groundless. Children usually accept parents as they are, and what matters to other people is not physical age (appearances can be notoriously deceptive anyway), but attitudes and outlook and readiness to relate as a caring father to young children.

There really does seem to be something in the belief that children 'keep you young'. Men who, with grown-up children, might slump into the slothful, sedentary existence that often comes with middle-aged prosperity, *have* to remain lively and outward-looking to cope with the demands of young children – games in the park, swimming at the weekend, school activities – not to mention the demands of a younger spouse. As for the prosperity that often enables middle-aged men, with their children 'off their hands', to live in comfort with expensive cars and frequent holidays abroad, that can be no more than a wistful pipe-dream for the second-time father, who is faced with expensive demands from his young family in terms of housing, transport and upbringing, often with only one salary coming in.

Christobel, 31, married to Gavin, 46, says that she thinks an older man makes a different kind of father. 'He is patient, interested, he adores them. He is also in awe of me for having had them; he is aware of everything I went through. I don't think a younger man would be capable of such a feeling. Younger men walk out of a relationship and forget the children. They don't think, I can't leave her because she had my children for me.'

John Mortimer, the writer, who inherited four stepdaughters with his first marriage to Penelope Mortimer, had two with her, and then had another child in his second marriage, writes of the joys of late fatherhood, of the preciousness of the child born in later life. 'The child of middle age is so greatly loved because you can see much more clearly the limit set on your time together.'

For many older fathers, confidence in themselves and in their child-rearing ability makes older parenthood more rewarding. 'I think when I was younger I was very hung up on the "shoulds" and "shouldn'ts" – you know, children should behave like this or like that, they should be reading by such and such an age, all that. Now I just think that Freddie is Freddie and will do things at his own pace . . . I don't push him to achieve at school like I did the children of my first marriage.'

Tim, too, thinks that he is a better father second time around. 'Being older, we really thought through the decision to have a child, whereas first time it just sort of happened. I am more mature, I have gone through more of life's experiences, so I think I have more insight and awareness into the effects on the child of what we're doing. I have so much more patience with Max than I did with my first family. I didn't see so much of them – I was out pursuing my career, going to conferences and staying late. Now I get to the end of the day and I just want to come home to help with bathtime, read a story and see Max before he goes to bed. That's really the most important thing in my day.'

Geoffrey, 56, had two children from his first marriage, now grown up, and three in his marriage with his 18-years-younger wife. 'My first marriage was a bit of a disaster,' he says, 'we were never really close. I think this had an effect on the children and on my relationship with them. Because I was unhappy I was more wrapped up in myself and because my ex-wife and I did not have a good physical relationship, that rubbed off on the children. I feel as if I'm more intimate with my children now because I'm more intimate with my wife. There is a different quality to the whole marriage and that has made me a different kind of father.'

For others, late parenthood can be a problem, not just for the father, but the wife and children as well. This is especially the case where a man has not had children before and has got used to life without them. 'I had my career and was very self-confident and in control, and then suddenly this little baby came along and I wasn't in control any more. I never knew when he was going to wake up, when he was going to cry, which days my wife would be happy and which days she'd ring me at work saying she couldn't stand it and would I come home early. We couldn't go out any more, we couldn't invite friends over, my wife was constantly tired and irritable. I just hadn't anticipated what it would be like. Everything was turned completely upside-down.'

Another older father confessed, 'When you've been for a long time with no children, it is a terrible shock. You're just not used to this invasion of your time and the lack of privacy and the constant demands for trivial things. And also I didn't realise it would be so exhausting. Maybe this is where younger men score. I found for months on end we'd never go out and never do anything because sleep was so precious that nothing in the world was worth a late night.'

Sometimes these are just teething troubles; but for some older men, the problems continue. 'I suppose as I get older I just want some peace and quiet,' says Geoffrey, who had two children in his first marriage and another two in his second. 'I think the first time round I had more energy. I was working longer hours than I am now, but when I was home with the kids I used to knock a ball round the garden with them for hours, taking them swimming or bike riding or play endless board games. This time I just can't do it. I've been through it all before.'

Geoffrey thinks that attitudes to parenthood have changed a lot in the 20 years that separate his first family from his second. 'Nowadays my wife, Judith, works part-time, which my first wife didn't do till the kids were at school. This means that she has less time for shopping and cooking so I have to take over some of that too. I have to get home early two evenings a week and put the kids to bed because Judith works late. This means I have a different relationship with the children – closer, yes, which is a good thing, but I also resent it a bit. I didn't think that at the age of 55 I'd be spending my spare time wiping bottoms and reading endless versions of Thomas the Tank-Engine.'

It's your baby

Jo, who had a daughter by her older husband, says that she feels she bears the brunt of parenting. 'First, this was because he had had two children before and it was always understood that this was "my" baby. I found there were fewer arguments if I just got on and did it all, so I didn't complain. There was a stage when Amy wouldn't go to him very readily because she just wasn't used to being with him and I did point out what was happening and that in the end he'd lose out. He is quite good with her now, he plays games and doesn't ask a lot. I think that's one area in which older fathers score; they are much more accepting of what people are. He's not always pushing her or wanting her to be what she's not, as some younger fathers seem to be.

'I do see younger fathers with their children and they seem to have more energy. Some friends of ours came the other day, he is 37 with two boys, and he takes them out to activities, rushes around with them, is bursting with life and enthusiasm. Perhaps that's just his character, I've no doubt that there are some 37-year-old fathers who just slump in front of the television, but I'm sure there is a big difference because of his age.'

Charlie Chaplin's son from his first marriage, Charles Junior, has written that Chaplin seemed much more at ease with babies than in the days when he and his brother had been infants, but the other son from his first marriage, Michael, noted that 'When you're 72 and you believe that you've had all the experiences . . . it's maybe a little tough to try to start playing the "my boy and I are just great pals" type of father.' Whatever kind of father he was, Charlie Chaplin was certainly prolific, fathering three children by his first wife and having a further eight children after the age of 54 in his marriage to Oona, the last fathered in his seventies.

Teenage turbulence

Does the generation gap between older fathers and their teenage children make for problems in the turbulent teenage years? Sarah, whose children are 13 and 15, thinks that it doesn't. 'Actually, I think that they respect him. Perhaps it's because his generation saw things differently and he's always been much stricter with the children than I have. I think, too, that they see that he is a respected person in the outside world, somebody to whom people come for advice. So perhaps they see him as a kind of wise old man. On the other hand, I have to cope with a lot of the problems which are offloaded on to me because I'm closer to them and I'm there much more than he is.' Obviously it helps to talk about what kind of roles you'll have with the children and how much you expect your partner will help.

Gillian thinks the age gap does make for problems. 'He is just much further away from them in terms of age and interests than many of the fathers I see,' she says. 'He's also got very laid back now that he's older and he doesn't bother with them so much. He just says, 'Oh, let them get on with it, they'll grow out of it,' and goes on potting his geraniums. I'm sure he's right in a way, after all he's seen his first family go through the same thing and emerge all right the other side, but I find it infuriating, because in practice it means he's abdicating all responsibility to me.'

Destructive criticism

Sometimes resentment about an older father's distance from the children can have a destructive effect. As Gillian says, 'One day when I was putting my eldest son to bed he asked me, "Why is Daddy so old? Is he going to die soon?" He's been hearing it all the time – "You boring old man, why don't you go and play football with them,", "You're too old to do that," and so on. I suddenly realised what I was doing and vowed that I would be very careful what I said in front of the children from then on.'

Some wives of older men do blame many things their husbands do on their age, but don't realise that wives with younger husbands often make exactly the same criticisms of their partners. 'I remember spending a weekend with a friend's family while my husband was away,' says Liz, 38, whose husband is 55. 'I was amazed to see that her 40-year-old husband was just as boring as mine!'

Another issue which concerns some women is that their circle of friends tends to be older – often the husband's age – and therefore they do not usually have young children. 'I found I had to make an extra effort to make friends with other mothers,' says Yvonne. 'We get on fine when it comes to the children but I never try to get together with the husbands because they would have nothing in common and I know it wouldn't work.'

There can be practical problems, too. Parents who might like to opt for private education, especially at secondary level, or who will have to pay for further education, may find that once the husband is retired he is unable to meet the costs. Making plans for the future and investing money for when it will be needed may make life easier later on.

What do the children make of it? Marjorie, whose husband is 56, doesn't think it matters at all. 'I don't think it means much to the children. My husband looks 10 years younger than he is and doesn't look much different from the other fathers at the school gates. He cycles to work and is very fit and healthy, so there's no reason to think he'll die before the children cease to need him.'

Robert has rather a different story. His father was 20 years older than his mother. 'I suppose that it was when I was about 10 that I first realised my father was much older than my mother. Before then it didn't matter; he was just Daddy. But I realised that he couldn't play rough and tumble games with me and that he used to take a long time to do things. Then I spent most of my teenage years worrying that he would die before I was grown up, which he finally did, when I was 17. It wasn't the loss of him that was so bad as what it did to my mother; I don't think I saw her smile for nearly two years.'

One fear which many older fathers have is that if anything happened to their wife, they would have to bring up the children on their own, despite their advancing years. An extreme case is that of a couple who had quads following fertility treatment; she was 40, he was 70. How would he cope if anything happened to his younger wife? If she died this would leave the children with the almost certainty of being orphaned before they are grown up. The importance of making a will which makes provision for such a situation, appointing suitable guardians and making sure there will be enough money, cannot be over stressed.

Chapter 7

MARRIAGE AS TIME GOES BY

Crabbed age and youth cannot live together:
Youth is full of pleasance, age full of care.

WILLIAM SHAKESPEARE,
The Passionate Pilgrim

How do marriages of older men and younger women fare as the years go by? Does the age gap become more important? Are the differences examined in earlier chapters even more pronounced – or do couples learn to live with them?

The royal marriage between Prince Charles and Lady Diana Spencer provides a classic example of how a couple can drift apart, and how the generation gap can make problems. While their marriage obviously suffers from many pressures which do not affect ordinary people, some young wives of older men will find common areas of discord.

Lady Diana was barely 20 when she married; Prince Charles was 12 years her senior. At first, they appeared very much in love; although when the engagement was announced and Charles was asked if he was in love, he replied: 'Yes – whatever love means.' The age gap was mentioned, and Charles is quoted as saying, 'You're only as young as you think you are. Diana will keep me young.' After their fairy tale wedding, the young princess seemed to smarten up her husband and help him grow more in touch with the values of his own generation.

Although two sons were born and Diana adapted very well to her new role and status, within a few years, problems started to emerge. Some felt that public adulation had gone to the Princess's head. Charles became increasingly introverted. Private rows became public. The Princess started to go out and about increasingly without Charles, enjoying the company of young and famous friends while he became increasingly reclusive. Charles' biographer Anthony Holden writes 'The twelve year gap between them began to tell . . . Diana found Charles' contemporaries boring, while he found hers very naive.'

Holden's analysis is that the young, naive and infatuated 19-year-old married a James Bond style prince, the 'world's most eligible bachelor with looks and lifestyle to match', and found herself married to a self-doubting introvert, uncertain of his role. All they had in common was their children, and Charles was seeing increasingly less of them.

By October 1987, the tabloids were having a field day. The royal couple had spent almost the entire summer holidays apart. There were headlines like: 'Charles and Diana not speaking' and 'Are Charles and Di moving apart?' There was even speculation about the possibility of a royal divorce.

However, since they were no ordinary couple, divorce has so far not been an option. More recent revelations have shown that, despite a public accommodation, they face real difficulties together.

This kind of problem is more likely to emerge if the younger wife is very young when she marries. A girl of 19 or 20 has a lot of growing up to do. What she feels for an older man may be an infatuation; it may be a way of escaping from a drab or ordinary existence into a world which otherwise might seem quite inaccessible; it may be based on unrealistic ideas of romantic love. As the years pass and reality intrudes, she may become dissatisfied and unhappy.

One woman wrote: 'I married a man 25 years older than I, 44 years ago. In a few days he will be 95. My advice to any woman contemplating marriage with such an age gap is: Don't.'

Amanda was 21 when she married her 38-year-old husband. He was a successful banker, and had money and a lifestyle to match; she had been his secretary. Youthful and good-looking, he turned her head; and all her friends envied her. The couple had two children, could afford nannies, and lived stylishly.

But 12 years later the marriage is in trouble. Amanda is 33, her husband 50. 'He has put on weight, and he still works all the time. All he wants to do is come home for dinner and watch TV or a video and he has become utterly boring,' says Amanda. Now that the children are a bit older she finds herself with nothing much to do; she has considered going back to work but, 'We don't need the money'. She wants to travel and do new things; he has done them all. She finds herself increasingly seeing her friends on her own and is making plans to go on holiday with them rather than with her husband. If she met a man her age who attracted her she would be very tempted to have an affair.

Some marriages are not happy from the beginning, as was the case for Geraldine: 'I first met my husband when I was about 14 and he was 31. He was a teacher at the school where my father was deputy head and he came to our house once. I met him again 10 years later at a school play and we had a whirlwind romance. He proposed within the week. I'm ashamed to admit it, but I accepted because I saw it as a way of breaking off an affair with a married man. I saw Jim as a trustworthy, solid sort of person and I thought I could grow to love him; after all I did like him.

'We had two children – Jim didn't want any more. I never did fall in love with him, which probably led to me being less forgiving about his faults than I should be. We used to have dreadful rows and many's the time I've wanted to leave, but I didn't want to hear all the 'I told you so's.' I couldn't bear to have any further physical relationship with him after a hysterectomy at the age of 36, and Jim promised that he'd never force me into sex if only I'd stay.

'I think the most disappointing thing about marrying an older man has been that he saw marriage as his ultimate goal, whereas for me it was a new start. A man at 40 plus has already achieved most of what he'll ever achieve, a woman of 24 still has a lot ahead of her, and I feel that we've not really *shared* our lives.'

Motives for marriage

Dr Emmanuel Lewis of the Tavistock Institute says that a woman who married a man over 40 who has not been married before should perhaps think carefully about why he has not done so. It is sufficiently unusual for a prospective wife to wonder why. Is he perhaps a Don Juan type who has had lots of affairs – and may have more? Does he have homosexual leanings or has he ever been a practising homosexual? Is he afraid of commitment? Why does he want to marry now?

Bridget was 36 when she met Robin, a bachelor at 50. 'I knew he had had a long-standing relationship with a married woman who was a Catholic and so wouldn't consider leaving her husband. I shouldn't have taken this at face value; I should have asked him a bit more. I suppose at 36 I was getting desperate to marry because I wanted to have a child. He was good-looking, charming and intelligent.

'After we married I realised that he wasn't interested in having a normal married life. When we tried, nothing happened; it seemed he just didn't find me attractive. He told me he was not homosexual but I don't know. I left him after six months; it was terrible admitting to everyone how wrong I had been.'

Marriages with big age gaps can partly founder from lack of support from family and friends. Marriage is a difficult institution at the best of times, and most couples can benefit from the help that intimates give. In age-gap marriages friends are also usually from different generations and tend to retain their loyalty to the friend they once knew rather than to the couple, thus pulling couples apart rather than welding them together.

Jim, married to a woman 18 years younger, recalls: 'When my first marriage broke up all our friends were shocked and said, 'But you can't, you seem to get on together so well, you have so much in common.' Our break-up was disruptive to them, too. It meant that a whole pattern of life – going to visit one another, sharing the children – was under threat. When things started to get difficult in my second marriage, the same old friends said. 'She's flighty; you're better off without her. You shouldn't have married her in the first place.'

What makes a marriage work?

Psychiatrist Anthony Storr writes of the concept of 'mature dependence'; he argues that one aspect of mature relationships seems to be the avoidance of either dominating or being dominated by the other person. This may be harder to achieve where one partner – here the husband – is older, maturer, more wealthy or more powerful; or where a younger wife holds power through her youth, health and attractiveness to men.

In some marriages between older men and younger women there is a very powerful dynamic going on. Two people who detest each other are closer emotionally than if they were detached. Often people hate in other people some quality which they dislike in themselves. There are some relationships between older men and younger women where the man exerts a dominant influence over the woman. The woman sees herself as a victim, trapped by the older, dominant man. Despite the many reasons given as to why she can't leave him, it is obvious that in most cases the woman is getting something out of the relationship; these days, divorce is always available as a solution to a bad marriage.

Barbara married a man who was 23 years older; she was 27, he was 49. They met through work – he was managing director of the company they worked for. She says that none of the things she feared about marrying him actually happened. Firstly, her children were not aware of having an older father; 'He seemed younger than his years, and blended in well during nursery and school, looking no older than the other daddies and considerably younger than some. And he did not leave them orphans at an early age; my daughter was 30 and my son 37 when he died.'

But Barbara's marriage was not happy. 'If anyone should ever try to tell you that hell is something you might, if you were unlucky, experience after death, they lie. Hell is here on earth, I was made to live it, every moment of every day for 37 years.'

Barbara says when she met her husband, she was a war widow and very vulnerable. She says that he was a difficult man, with a Jekyll and Hyde character; 'At first, I thought he was kind, but he turned out to be the cruellest man I ever knew. He couldn't bear to see anyone happy.' Why did she never leave him? 'I would have run if I had the chance but you can't with no money and two children. He was determined that I should never get away from him. When he died I was very glad to see the back of him. He was a horror.'

For other women it is not the whole marriage which is a disaster but the end of it. Paula met her husband at a Christmas party; 'I had just had my twenty-fifth birthday and my future husband was 50. I found him extremely attractive, lots of fun and exciting. My family were bitterly opposed to the marriage except for my brother, with whom I was very close – he did not exactly approve but he supported me.'

The couple lived abroad because of her husband's work. 'The first few years were all right but I began to realise that the man I had married in England was a totally different person out here. I will not go into details. Just recalling my life gives me a headache.

'Age differences have never meant anything to me. I have friends young enough to be my daughters. It is the mind that matters. But when one is 25, one never can imagine being 70 and having to look after a 95 year old. His mind (what he had of it) has gone. We have no conversation; nothing sinks in. I have ended up as the matron, cook-housekeeper, chauffeuse, secretary, nurse, etc. My opinion is that age differences do not matter in the beginning but become unbearable in great old age.'

Divorce

Statistics show that second marriages are more likely to end in divorce than first marriages. Since many older men have been married before, the odds must be higher against some of these marriages working out. Divorce is the ultimate recourse in a failed marriage, and can be even more painful and messy than a first break-up.

If a woman leaves an older man she is likely to feel guilt. 'I felt terrible leaving him because I was afraid he was too old to find happiness with anyone else,' says Marianne. 'I felt I'd be leaving him to cope alone in his old age.'

Janet married a man 12 years older. She felt the marriage had failed, they had grown apart and no longer had anything in common. 'He never did anything with me, never came on holiday with me and the children, was only interested in his work.' She had actually left her husband at 50 and had initiated divorce proceedings when he suffered a heart attack. 'He was very ill and needed surgery. Of course, I went back and nursed him through it. When he was recovered and in good health again I said I wanted to live apart but agreed I wouldn't actually divorce him, as there wasn't another man involved and I didn't want to remarry.

'After a year he had a second heart attack. He hung on for some time after another lot of surgery, but finally died in hospital. I was with him, holding his hand. I am now glad that I didn't divorce him and saw it through; I was aware of how much I'd helped him. But guilt still stays with me.'

Sometimes the boot is on the other foot and it is the wife who is shocked by her husband wanting to end the marriage. When the husband leaves the younger wife for another woman – often one still younger – she can feel doubly betrayed. 'I asked myself, what's wrong with me? Aren't I good enough?' says Jenny, 35, whose husband, 48, left her for a woman in her twenties after eight years of marriage. 'The stupid thing was that I felt so secure with him. I compared my marriage to that of my other friends and I thought, he won't leave me, he's already got somebody younger. What is he after that I can't provide? My only consolation is that it's unlikely to last with her either – probably in another few years he'll run off with a 19 year old.'

All the practical problems of divorce remain the same as for first time round, but there can be complications. 'When I married Derek, I inherited his daughter Lily from his first marriage, who was then five. Then we had one of our own. The two girls are inseparable, so when Bob and I split up I had custody of them both. Bob complained bitterly; he said, after all,

Lily wasn't anything to do with me. So now I have to deal with her grandparents, Bob's former wife's family, directly myself. The family relationships are very complicated.'

Divorce is always a traumatic event for both partners, even where one or both feel that it is the only solution – indeed, even where at least one partner has already formed a new liaison to fill the void.

Fortunately, more marriages endure than disintegrate, even though there will almost inevitably be other problems to deal with as the years go by.

Failing potency

One fear that older husbands face is that their wives might seek sexual relationships with younger men, especially if sexual attraction is fading. Alice said her husband need not have worried about this. 'I felt an enormous sexual attraction to Joe from the very start and the main reason that I have been faithful is that I have never met anyone else since who has made me feel that way. We still enjoy an active sex life 25 years after marriage; we're now aged 50 and 69.'

However, in some marriages, especially if there is ill-health, this can be a problem. Vicky was 24 when she married Kevin, who was 46. 'Our marriage was fine for about 15 years. We had two children and enjoyed life. Then Kevin had his first coronary and bypass surgery. I thought he was going to die; he did come fairly close. After that things were never the same. Although the bypass worked, he now sees himself as a bit of an invalid. He doesn't want to go out anywhere and do much and I do. I feel I'm getting older, too. But I'm still attractive, and I want to enjoy myself while I can – and while men still find me desirable.'

'I have had affairs. I need to be loved, appreciated, I want some of the wild sex I used to have but which Kevin and I are now afraid of. I've told Kevin I'll never leave him and I won't; I do love him. But if I didn't have other men I would be irritable and horrible to him. I'm not horrible to him at all, when I'm with him I'm very devoted. Perhaps it's because I feel guilty too.'

Facing up to retirement

People's approach to retirement differs widely, whether they take this early – due to ill-health or the nature of their work – or are able to continue working long past the usual age. Given good health and a comfortable financial situation, it can be a very happy and fulfilling time, with opportunities to expand one's range of leisure interests and make new social contacts.

If the possibilities (not necessarily probabilities) are considered ahead of time, you can make contingency plans – plans which, with luck, you may never need to put into operation. Just knowing you are prepared for any eventuality can be enormously reassuring and leave you free to enjoy life together without always worrying about the future.

Chris is one of the lucky ones who has been able to continue working way past usual retirement age. But he is now 70 and at last has slowed down just sufficiently to think about the future. His wife is 24 years younger, and he says that their marriage has been very happy. They had two children and both partners work. 'But I shall retire next year and I wonder if that will make any difference to our relationship. One of its great strengths is that we've always been quite independent; my work takes me out in the evenings and away on tours. I hope being at home isn't going to change all that.'

Jo found retirement brought problems; she met her husband Matthew when she was 30 and he was 48. 'I didn't really notice the age gap at all. I'd just finished my degree, and was embarking on a teaching course. Matthew was head of the art department and I thought he looked attractive. We fell in love. He was married at the time, but the marriage was in a bad state – he and his wife had had separate bedrooms for six years – and he moved out to live with me.

'I think part of me was attracted to his status and money. I had been a single parent for 10 years, and he had a big house, two successful daughters, money. I loved the whole package – but of course I never got it. We moved in here and had our daughter Alice, who is now 6 years old. I would have liked another child, but just having one was part of the deal.

'Matthew took early retirement two years ago, so now we are quite hard up. I do most of the parenting and now I suppose I will have to be the main breadwinner. I have turned 40 myself and I feel that we are beginning to move into that faceless middle age, where having an older husband doesn't help.

'I think when I was 30 and he was 48, we both seemed quite young. At 40 and 58, I see more problems. What worries me is what it will be like when I'm 50 and he's 68. I mean, 68 is quite old. One starts worrying about all those diseases that affect older people. I heard a talk on the radio the other day and it said that senile dementia affects one person in 10 over the age of 60. It sounds dreadful to talk about it, there's no reason why that should affect Matthew, but I suppose it's something we ought to think about.

'On the whole things have worked out well. There isn't anyone else I've met I would rather be with. But marriage is difficult enough at the best of times, without having a big age-gap to add to the problems. My father is eight years older than my mother and while I never noticed it when I was younger I notice it now, and it's going to show more and more. And that's only eight years; what about 18? I didn't think about this when I married, but I do think about it now. It's the future that bothers me. I am aware and conscious of it in a way that I wasn't before.'

When serious illness strikes

Some younger women accept that they may have 10 or 20 good years, and that they may then have to pay for it. Some resent this, but others do not mind.

Heather married at 30 a man 24 years older than herself. They had two children; she didn't have to work, was comfortably off, enjoyed holidays abroad and never had financial or other worries. But when she was 50, it became apparent that John, now aged 74, was suffering from a form of premature senility. She does not resent this and cares for him herself at home.

'I knew when I married that something like this might happen,' she says. 'Of course, I hoped that he would remain fit and healthy into his eighties like other men I know, but this is bad luck. After all, it is an illness, it might have happened in his sixties or fifties, I might have had the same problem if I'd married a man my own age, though I suppose this is less likely. But I had 20 good years. When the children were young, I was the envy of many of my friends who were struggling to make ends meet and didn't have the advantages that I had. We've had a good marriage, so now I don't mind paying back some of the good things John has given me in the past.'

Not everyone is so mature – or so loving. Sarah, 38, married a man 20 years her senior. He has had a heart problem and is not in good health. 'I am stuck,' she says. 'I go out on my own, he won't come on holiday with me. We are always talking about his health or whether he can do this or that. I try to lead as separate a life as possible and I have had one or two short affairs. I wouldn't tell him; he'd be upset. I pretend to him that things are better than they are.

'Why do I stay with him? Guilt, I suppose. He is so sweet to me. He always says he doesn't want to get in my way, he wants me to enjoy myself, he trusts me, he wants the best for me. Actually, the best thing he could do for me right now would be to just drop dead.'

The contrast between these two women and their marriages points to areas which account for success and failure in any relationship.

For women who marry an older man, it helps to be aware that things will change as you both get older, and those who try to deal with these changes in a positive manner, rather than letting them undermine the relationship, will fare much better. When things go wrong it is all too easy to blame it on the man's age rather than on other problems, especially those to do with yourself. Professional counselling can help get things out into the open and provide a basis for sorting out problems which, unresolved, can destroy your marriage and your happiness, whether you stay together or not.

Chapter 8

WIDOWED BEFORE TIME

'I can't bear to think that one of us will have to die first.'

'Nor can I.'

'Let's not think about it.'

You say that when you are first in love, first married; then as the years pass you stop saying it, because you are forced to think about it.

BEL MOONEY,
The Penguin Book of Marriage

Women who marry older men know when they do so that there is an increased risk of their partner dying some time before they do. Since women usually outlive men, an age gap of 10 years or more means that the woman can – on average – expect many years of widowhood.

Of course, since life expectancy has increased so dramatically and since medical advances can ensure a longer and more active life for those who suffer from serious diseases such as heart disease or cancer, even women who marry a man in his fifties or sixties can reasonably expect 15-20 happy years together, as much as many younger couples can expect before divorce. And widowhood is inevitable for most women, whether they have married a younger man or not.

Women who marry older men may not be much worse off than average women. In the United States, the median age when widowhood occurs is 56 years; three out of four American wives can expect to become widows, and there are about six times as many widows as widowers. Only about one-fourth of all widows remarry, as against half of all widowers, but younger widows are statistically much more likely to remarry.

At the time of marriage, few people look very far into the future. As one woman married to a man nearly 20 years older said, 'For us it was really love. I wasn't going to throw away my present happiness – a happiness that could easily last 20 or 30 years – because of some vague fears about what might happen in the distant future.'

Ann was 27 when she married and her husband had just turned 40. 'I was shy, meek, totally lacking in self-confidence and had always been protected by my family. It was an attraction of opposites for me – no two people could have been more different and yet we complemented one another in so many ways. It was many years later that I realised how much he must have loved me – protecting me and lavishing care and counsel on me – culminating in the changing of his whole life and philosophy to accommodate mine. I had no fears from the very beginning, but I think he wondered whether he could maintain the change in life he had adopted. He did and, over the years, we moved ever closer together until we thought and acted more or less in unison.

'The difference in our ages had no significance until he retired. Then he seemed to age very quickly and expected me, at 50, to look, talk and act as his contemporary. The difference in our ages was exacerbated by the fact that by the time he was 70, he had contracted cancer and fought bravely against it for five years. When he died I was 62 and bereft. No, I have no regrets at having married an older man – just sorrow that we could not have had more years together. Why was it so long before we found each other?'

When death is sudden

If the death of the partner is sudden, it can be an even greater shock: Rachel and Harold had five happy years together. 'Then, in January, 1981, I came home from school on the second day of term to find my husband lying dead on the floor. He was 66; I was 38. He had died soon after lunch, quite alone, from a heart attack. There was a post-mortem, lots of questions from a very young policeman, but no inquest.

'At the time I took it all very calmly but, inside, I was devastated. My periods stopped for two years (no physical reason, just shock). About a month after he died my throat and upper chest became very painful. I thought it was an emotional reaction. It was pleurisy. I had a month off work, and when I returned I felt like a new recruit; all my confidence had gone.

'There seemed to be no reason for me to live. I wanted to be dead too, but I didn't consider suicide, not wanting to upset my family – who are Roman Catholics and would have been horrified.'

Women who are widowed young have far more difficulty than those who are widowed in their sixties, seventies or later. Susan Wallbank, a counsellor for CRUSE, the national organisation for the widowed and their children, says that women who are widowed in their fifties are hit particularly hard. 'For them, widowhood takes place in a no man's land. They are not young, they are not old; they fall between these two identifiable categories.'

A young widow usually receives massive support from family and friends, and is young enough to start life over again. Often, she will remarry, as did Rachel, above. For a woman in her fifties, life is more difficult. Says Susan Wallbank, 'Often her children have just left home – she is losing the role of mother. Her parents may be ageing and need care, and she is taking on again the role of daughter. It is a very confusing time for her. If she loses the role of wife as well, it can be devastating.'

CRUSE finds that proportionally more women in their fifties contact them than any other age group. 'I think these women experience a specific kind of loneliness. Most couples in their

fifties are looking forward to retirement, to their children becoming independent, to reaping the rewards of the hard work
they have put in over the years. If – when you are within reach of
this future you've planned – your partner dies, you feel robbed,
that your future has been stolen from you.

'Often, in their fifties couples are coming closer together,'
continues Susan Wallbank. 'A woman widowed in her fifties
often finds that all her friends are closely wrapped up in their
partners; this reinforces her own loneliness and isolation.' Unlike a woman in her sixties or seventies, she does not know many
other widows to befriend or do things with. She is too young to
have grandchildren with whom to become involved and children
are often at the stage of being most independent, before marriage when children will bring them back more into the family
orbit.'

Susan Wallbank also thinks that there are particular problems
for widows of older partners. 'Women who have married older
men are often aware that they are different from others. This
difference makes it harder for them to find people who are in the
same situation or who understand.'

Christine, whose partner died aged 71, when she was only 52,
says, 'People said things like, "Well, you must have expected it,"
as though this made it easier. Of course I didn't expect it. He died
suddenly from a heart attack. I didn't expect it any more than I
would have expected it if my husband had been in his fifties like
myself, only then people would have had more sympathy.'

Greater dependency

Another problem for some younger widows is that in such
relationships there may be an extra element of dependency.
Elizabeth sums this up well. 'There were 18 years between
Richard and me. He looked after me completely. He dealt with
all the financial things and he made sure that money worries and
other things didn't affect me. He used to buy things for me and
spoil me. He also made all the decisions about things like
holidays, booking it all up as a surprise for me. So when he died,

I was absolutely devastated. I couldn't cope with anything. I didn't know what to do.'

Some younger women have married older men precisely because the older man gives them this sense of security; it is harder then to cope alone. In addition, many wives of older men find that they have, in a sense, 'moved up a generation'; their friends are often older and they move in a social circle to which they belong by virtue of their partner's age. Then, when they are on their own, they don't belong there any more; but neither do they feel they any longer belong to their own generation, who will not on the whole have had the same life experiences.

Marilyn was devastated when her husband died at the age of 70, leaving her in her late fifties. 'The children had all left home. The last one finished at university two years ago and lived with me for just a year, while looking for jobs in London. So, I lost all my children and my husband at the same time. Although there had been difficulties in the marriage in the last few years – due to Ronald becoming increasingly stick-in-the-mud and me wanting to travel, and then because of his illnesses – I wasn't prepared for how I would feel.

'First, I discovered that none of my friends understood. They were all busy with their own lives and husbands and soon got tired of listening to me. Other people said, "Well at least he won't be a burden to you," or "Isn't it all for the best?" and that kind of thing, which I didn't find at all helpful.'

Another widowed woman in her fifties said that she felt some of her friends actually viewed her as a threat. 'I was still very attractive when I was widowed at 48 and I'm sure a lot of people thought that I was out to steal their husbands. Also, I think those whose husbands were a bit older didn't like to be reminded that the same thing might happen to them, so they tended to avoid me. I also got fed up with being asked along to dinner parties and tacked on as a spare wheel.'

Everyone who has been widowed comments that after the initial support they feel they have been stigmatised. People who were previously friendly and approachable are embarrassed or strained in the widow's presence. Expressions of sympathy are given but may begin to sound hollow. Offers of help may be made but not followed up. Usually, only those who share in the loss are able to offer support. The widow often feels she has been tainted with death, as if she might pass it on to others. In some more 'primitive' societies widows are isolated or even made to commit ritual suicide.

As we have already seen, younger widows are often hit much harder. Colin Murray Parkes, in his classic study, *Bereavement*, found that whereas widows under the age of 65 frequently consulted their GPs for help with emotional problems during the first six months after bereavement, this was not the case with older widows.

One woman quoted in his book grieved intensely for several years after the death of her husband – at the age of 35 she had married a man 18 years her senior. After his retirement 12 years later, he became totally bound up with his home, his garden and with her. He hated it when she went out to work. In the last 10 years he had begun to show his age and she nursed him through his last illness. As he relied on her more and more, she spent less time away from him and if she did go to visit friends or relatives was always in a hurry to be back. Her husband's death deprived her of her main role in life, but also left her socially isolated and feeling she had failed to 'preserve' him.

Another case of grief cited by Parkes is that of a woman of 28 who married a man 20 years her senior. She had been a nervous and timid woman, but enjoyed her role as wife, although sadly she and her husband did not have children. 'From the first our relationship was absolutely ideal – it was so right. I seemed to find myself. He was in hospital for six weeks and returned home only to have a stroke and die that very night.' This was after 11 years of being very happily married.

When he died, she 'did not stop crying for months . . . And for years I couldn't believe it, I can hardly believe it now.' She finds it hard to get on with other women: 'They've got homes, husbands and children. I'm alone and they're not.'

When an older husband dies leaving young children, the widow has to cope with their grief as well as her own. Their presence can make things easier for her, in that she has the comfort of the children to hold and care for, but also more difficult, in that these responsibilities may hinder the process of her own grief. Sarah, whose husband was 18 years older and died leaving her with two boys aged seven and nine, recalls: 'The boys, of course, were shattered. I spent all the time trying to shield them from my grief and making sure that life went on more or less as usual. The result was that I didn't grieve properly myself. I couldn't really let myself go and howl and rage as I wanted to; I couldn't express my anger at Keith being taken away from me. I was frightened of what I might do if I let go and how this would affect the children.'

The process of grief

Grief takes many forms. It is now accepted that the process of grief usually has four distinct phases: Disbelief or denial, 'Tell me this isn't true; it can't have happened.' Then anger, 'Why me? Why did this happen?' Then there is a period of grief and mourning, and finally, acceptance.

People who are bereaved often have physical symptoms. They may feel alarmed, with symptoms which are very like fear, and they may often actually become ill. Research has shown that people are more prone to disease when suffering a bereavement. It is even possible actually to die of a 'broken heart.'

Often, bereaved people are restless, unable to settle, and exhibit behaviour in which they seem to be 'searching' for the lost person; they may even 'see' the person or 'hear' their voice. People search for their lost one's face in a crowd. Pangs of grief may be felt in the same way as a physical pain. The grief-stricken often think they are going mad, partly because we are not good at talking about death or what grief feels like, so we do not know what is normal.

Sometimes, the onset of grief is slower. The bereaved may be in shock initially. Others may experience more complicated emotions. Teresa's marriage had been in trouble for several years before her husband, Richard, who was 14 years older, died. She had been living apart from him until his last illness, when she came back to nurse him and was with him when he died. 'I felt sad because of all the things we had done together, but I suppose I was also relieved in a way because things hadn't been good and I was finally free. But then things started to happen. It was when I started tidying away his things, emptying his desk, getting rid of his clothes. I took out the suit he wore the day we married and remembered how I had felt about him then and the happy years we shared when the children were young. Perhaps, in a way, I was mourning my own youth. Death is just so terribly, terribly sad.'

Grief for a spouse can last for a long time. 'After a month or two people thought that I should have got over it and be getting back to normal. People who were sympathetic and listened to me at first soon melted away,' recalls Anne, who was widowed at 50. 'In particular, anniversaries were difficult: what would have been our 25th wedding anniversary, only six months after he died; his birthday; then, of course, the anniversary of his death. He died in March, so when the daffodils came up the following spring, I remembered driving to the crematorium and seeing them lining the road. So, the early signs of spring which usually bring cheer were unbearably sad for me.'

Jenny knew that she would find the anniversary of her husband's death difficult, so she arranged to spend it with her mother-in-law and her husband's son so that they could support one another through their grief. 'If I had tried to carry on as if it was a normal day, I would probably have broken down,' she recalls. 'As it was, we talked a lot about all the good aspects of George and his life and I felt much better.'

When women are widowed comparatively early in life they may find it difficult to find a new role for themselves. 'There is the merry widow and there is the grief-stricken wife,' says Paula. 'I wasn't comfortable with either role. Because Mark was 25 years older than me, and had been in poor health for some time, everybody assumed it must be a relief when he died. In a way it was; but that wasn't the point. I would much rather he had *not* been ill and *not* died'.

A younger widow's grief can be further complicated by relationships with the husband's former family, if he was married before. One second wife recalls the horror she experienced when she realised that her husband's first wife would attend the funeral. She says, 'I couldn't bear it. I thought of ringing her and begging her not to come, but I couldn't humiliate myself. Everybody said, be reasonable. She has a right to come, but you needn't speak to her. But I felt that in some way she would be taking over from me. I suppose we still feel that the first wife is somehow superior, she was the first, the 'real' wife. I couldn't bear the thought of her standing there smugly – she never really cared for him, it was she who instigated the divorce – while I was prostrated with grief. I knew that his daughters would stand with her and I felt they would somehow take over the whole occasion.'

This situation can be even worse if the second partner has a common law marriage and has not actually gone through an official ceremony. At Graham Greene's funeral, this meant the estranged wife took pride of place despite the fact that her husband had lived with another woman for many years.

Despite the frequency of divorce and remarriage today, these social problems have not yet been resolved; there is no established etiquette for such situations. No wonder people in such relationships can feel uneasy and unable to cope.

Financial problems

Many practical problems may also intrude at a time when the woman is experiencing her loss. Janet was 24 when she married her husband, aged 36, and they had five children together. He died at the age of 51, when she was 39, and they had five children at school or university. She discovered, to her horror, that her husband's pension and life assurance provisions were inadequate, and being under 50, she didn't qualify for a state widow's pension.

Margaret found that her husband's company pension scheme allowed them to pay the pension at a lower rate if a man's spouse was more than 10 years younger. 'I suppose they argued that they would be paying it out for longer, so they could give me less,' she says. 'I was devastated. I had counted on a certain amount of money, and I didn't get it. Although the children were through their schooling, they still needed help with things. My expenses are greater than they would have been if I had been the same age as my husband and, consequently, the children were of age when he died.'

This provision is found in many 'final salary' schemes, the type most commonly found in the public and private sectors. Usually, the rules give the trustees of the pension fund the discretion 'to reduce actuarially' the pension of a spouse more than 10 years younger than the member: this means that the bigger the age gap, the bigger the potential reduction. But trustees do not always exercise this option, and are unlikely to do so while there are dependent children. In a few schemes, the rules do not allow discretion, it is simply done. Other schemes do not have such a provision at all.

Again, some pension schemes will pay the widow a pension for life. But many will discontinue the pension if the widow remarries or even sets up a house with someone. And a few will only pay it until she starts drawing the State pension at 60. A letter to the fund trustees as soon as the marriage is reported to them, asking them to spell out the provisions of the scheme, should avoid the possibility of nasty shocks later.

Certainly an older husband, especially one with dependent children either born or intended, has a special responsibility to provide for his new family after his death, and the earlier he does so the less expensive this may be. Apart from sorting out his pension arrangements (may his ex-wife have claim on it?), the most important is the need for adequate life insurance, because he must face the possibility of dying before all his children have completed their education. There are all kinds of policies available to provide lump sums, family income for a specified period, and regular sums for children (which may be available not just for school fees, but to meet other expenses of a broadly educational nature), as well as annuities for the surviving spouse.

If a previous marriage has ended in divorce, it is preferable for the divorce settlement to be of the 'clean break' type, or an ex-wife might turn up years later with a claim on a life insurance pay-out, pension or even a family inheritance. A man who remarries must remake his will, and he may do this before hand (as soon as he is divorced) 'in contemplation' of remarriage.

Finally, it is worth remembering that 'actuarial probabilities' are not certainties: older men can and do outlive their wives. Philippa married Brian, 12 years her senior, at the age of 38. They had two boys. But she died of cancer at 51, when her sons were still at school, and Brian took early retirement to look after them.

Younger wives should give special thought to the extra funds that would be needed should *they* die with dependent children who have to be brought up by their older husband, perhaps already on a pension and with no means of increasing his income. Fortunately, this kind of protection is relatively cheap for younger women, and if it is written in the form of an endowment that matures when the youngest child completes his or her education, can then provide a useful capital sum for her own retirement. And it is worth remembering that endowment policies can also be a security for raising a loan, without actually cashing the policy in, if funds are temporarily needed. Widowed husbands can also get help from the social services if their need is great.

Financial considerations aside, the woman who has been widowed early has an opportunity to start again with her career, and to lead a fulfilling life. But many younger widows may be forced back into work, or feel the need to dedicate herself to some cause because she is denied the support usually offered by other widows.

Eva Loewe, a Jungian analyst, believes that many women married to older men are aware that they are going to have to stand alone one day and thus prepare themselves for when the time comes. It's a good idea for women married to older men to have some job or interest in which they can immerse themselves. Indeed, as we have already seen, a younger wife may have to have an income to supplement her husband's pension once he has retired.

But death is not just an end; it is also a new beginning. A marriage to an older man has as good a chance of being happy as any other marriage. A woman will fear or suffer her husband's loss in proportion to the amount that she has loved and gained from him. If she has prepared herself for life beyond the marriage she may have many years of fulfillment ahead, and even the chance of a second happy marriage.

USEFUL ADDRESSES

CRUSE
The National Organisation for the Widowed and their Children
126 Sheen Road
Richmond, Surrey
Tel: 081 940 4818
Offers a counselling service, advice and opportunities for social contact for all bereaved people and runs training courses for professional and lay people involved with the dying and bereaved

Family Planning Association
27-35 Mortimer Street
London W1N 7RJ
Tel: 071 636 7866
Information on sexuality, family planning and personal relationships

London Marriage Guidance Council
76a New Cavendish Street
Harley Street
London W1M 7LB
Tel: 071 580 1087
Counselling for those seeking help in marriage and other personal relationships

Relate – National Marriage Guidance
Herbert Gray College
Little Church Street
Rugby, Warwickshire CV21 3AP
Tel: 0788 73241
Counselling for those seeking help in marriage and other per-sonal relationships

Stepfamily – National Stepfamily Association
72 Willesden Lane
London NW6 7TA
Tel: 071-372 0844
Advice, information and counselling service for stepfamilies

WOOM
Wives of Older Men
1029 Sycamore Avenue
Tinton Falls
New Jersey 07724-3198
USA
Tel: (010 1 908) 747 5586
Founder: Beliza Ann Furman
Networking, information and support group with international membership

FURTHER READING

Families and How to Survive Them
Robin Skynner/John Cleese (Methuen 1983)

The Penguin Book of Marriage
Edited by Bel Mooney (Penguin 1991)

The Integrity of Personality
Anthony Storr (Pelican 1963)

Jennifer Fever: Older Men, Younger Women
Barbara Gordon (Harper & Row 1988)

Stepmotherhood: How to survive without feeling frustrated, left out or wicked
Cherie Burns (Piatkus 1987)

A Step-Parent's Handbook
Kate Raphael (Sheldon Press 1986)

Living with a Teenager
Suzie Hayman (Piatkus 1988)

Bereavement: Studies of Grief in Adult Life
Colin Murray Parkes (Pelican 1975)

Second Wife, Second Best
Glynnis Walker (Sheldon Press 1984)

Remarriage
Helen Franks (Bodley Head 1988)

Infertility: Modern treatments and the issues they raise
Maggie Jones (Piatkus 1991)

INDEX

Other Titles Published By Piatkus Books

He Says, She Says: *How to close the communication gap between the sexes* Dr Lillian Glass

The Passion Paradox: *What to do when one person loves more than the other* Dr Dean C Delis with Cassandra Phillips

Dare to Connect: *How to create confidence, trust and loving relationships* Susan Jeffers

For a free brochure with further information on our complete range of titles, please write to:

Piatkus Books
Freepost 7 (WD 4505)
London W1E 4EZ

PIATKUS